The Managing Director

The Managing Director

George Copeman

Now published by
BUSINESS BOOKS
24 Highbury Crescent
London N5 1RX

David & Charles
Newton Abbot   London   North Pomfret (Vt)   Vancouver

British Library Cataloguing in Publication Data

Copeman, George
  The managing director.
  1. Directors of corporations
  I. Title
  658.4'2   HF5500.2

ISBN 0–7153–7556–3

Library of Congress Catalog Card Number: 78–52161

Printed in Great Britain
by Redwood Burn Limited, Trowbridge and Esher
for David & Charles (Publishers) Limited
Brunel House Newton Abbot Devon

Published in the United States of America
by David & Charles Inc
North Pomfret Vermont 05053 USA

Published in Canada
by Douglas David & Charles Limited
1875 Welch Street North Vancouver BC

Contents

1

Who Sits in the Hot Seat?

In Britain there are more managing directors than coal miners. In round figures, there are only 240,000 mine workers but 600,000 registered companies, most of which have a managing director. The role of managing director provides more opportunity for people to exercise their talents than almost any other job.

Most companies are small and privately owned. There are only just over 1,000 British public companies listed on the Stock Exchange. However, a large company usually employs a considerable number of managing directors, for within the group each division and each subsidiary company may have its own MD.

When it comes to asking who is the typical managing director, there is no such person, but by far the greatest number of MDs are heads of small family businesses. Next in number are the heads of subsidiary firms within large companies. Most of these are career-minded managers promoted to the job, but a surprising number are former heads of family businesses which have been taken over.

Perhaps the élite among managing directors are the heads of medium-sized private firms with between 100 and 1,000 employees. They usually have more independence, more financial muscle, more standing in their own community than any other business group. If the company has been two or more generations in the same family, they have usually been educated at expensive schools and possibly at one of the more famous universities.

In a less attractive position are the managing directors of large public companies. They are mostly career-minded men without personal capital resources; they are answerable to a large body of shareholders, most of whom they may never meet, and in the larger companies they are sometimes over-shadowed by a chairman who may also be chief executive.

In a more exposed position are the heads of companies owned by government. They, too, are usually career-minded managers with little or no capital of their own. They are exposed to the normal criticisms of a managing director by customers, employees and suppliers, but in addition they are open to criticism in the Press and Parliament.

Managing directors of large companies generally have an academic or professional qualification, but thousands of smaller companies have MDs with no special scholastic back-ground. One of the most important characteristics of the role of managing director is that a person does not have to pass an examination to get the job. For this reason alone the MD's job provides career opportunities for many people who were dis-satisfied with their level of achievement at school. Having started out on their working careers with the sound of failure ringing in their ears, they were determined to prove that school was wrong in its judgement of them. They set about developing those hidden talents which had been overlooked and, in due course, proved themselves as self-made business-men, employing more people and handling more money than most of those who had outshone them in the classroom.

The role of managing director is a great leveller, but it levels up. It provides an opportunity for those who had an unhappy start to their careers to prove that, by working hard to provide some much-needed product or service, they can overtake their former classmates in the amount of money they earn and in the amount of personal capital they accumulate.

The MD's job does, however, involve financial risk. In Britain there are typically about 6,000 bankruptcies a year, the number varying greatly with economic conditions. In addition, many companies sack their managing director and appoint a new one when they experience a crisis, even though they may avoid actual bankruptcy.

Finally, a newly appointed managing director may fail in the job and be sacked before he has had a chance of seriously damaging the company. Usually his trouble is that he has been appointed too late in life and cannot make a successful jump from being number two, in charge of a single department, to being number one in overall charge. New habits and disciplines have to be learnt and the difficulty is that they must be learnt at double time, on the job. In spite of all the management training which goes on, the opportunity to become managing director very often falls unawares to someone who has had no specific training for the job.

What are the working methods and disciplines which a managing director must acquire if he is to make maximum use of his talents in the cause of running a successful business? This is the major question which we attempt to answer in this book. One thing can, however, be said in advance. Nobody should contemplate taking on the role of managing director unless he—or she—is a natural fighter who enjoys the unending excitement of coping with the problems of money and people. The responsibility for simultaneously serving the needs of customers and for creating wealth and employment, is not one to be undertaken lightly. This is possibly the most adult job available to all who can claim to be real triers. It offers a particular challenge to those who have been well educated at public expense and who have then found themselves landed with a boring, undemanding job which they cannot in their hearts justify as making a real contribution to society and which certainly does not put their full capabilities to the test.

Because the level at which a managing director works varies from company to company, we could be at risk in this book in trying to serve too many different needs with standard solutions. To give the book coherence, it is particularly necessary for both the author and the reader to have in mind the managing director of a specific size of firm.

We have chosen to overlook the special problems of the MD with just a few employees whose business is too small to have any need for delegation of major responsibilities. We have also chosen to neglect the special needs of the large-group MD who has probably had previous experience as managing director of a subsidiary company. The image which we have adopted is that of a head of a firm with about fifty employees, which is big enough to need the clear division of management into such functions as sales and production.

In most chapters of the book it will not make any difference whether the firm is owned by the managing director himself, by a number of private shareholders, by a large group or by the State. However, whenever there is an important distinction to be made between the interests of shareholders and those of the managing director, this will be indicated.

Finally, the book does not respect titles. We use the title of managing director to include that of executive chairman, chief executive, proprietor, president, general manager and all the other titles used by persons responsible for the overall management of a business.

2

Motivation by Money

If you are already a managing director or if you want to be one, then you should be strongly motivated by money and proud of that fact. An MD cannot do a good job in serving the public unless money excites him. This would seem to be obvious, but the detailed reasons for it have major significance.

A modern industrial democracy contains three different sectors which are responsible for satisfying people's various needs: the parliamentary sector, the club sector and the market sector. We need to look briefly at each of these in order to appreciate fully the role of money in the working life of a managing director.

The parliamentary sector receives most of the limelight and is sometimes treated as if it were the whole of democracy, although it is only one part. In Britain, the parliamentary sector handles an enormous flow of funds. Half the national income passes through the hands of central and local government departments.

The club sector includes the churches, trade unions, sports clubs, charities, scientific bodies and other organisations where people come together, as members, to pursue a specialised interest which may be shared in common by only a limited section of the population.

The market sector includes all business firms, whether

11

privately, co-operatively or State owned, or owned in some other way. The factor which distinguishes the market sector is not the type of ownership but the serving of customers. Over three-quarters of the working population are employed in this sector.

The differences between these three sectors of democracy are quite striking. Let us look firstly at the ways in which they reach decisions.

In the parliamentary sector people exercise their voting rights through the ballot box at election time. This has some influence on elected representatives and on public servants, but it is a remote and intermittent connection, though obviously important.

In the club sector people mostly vote with their feet. They may influence the policies of a society merely by joining or leaving it and by whether they participate in its activities. Most of them never vote at an electon of office-bearers.

In the market sector people vote with their purses, influencing decisions when they buy one product rather than another. Their influence is almost instantaneous and it is certainly continuous, if they are buying from day to day. The relationship between a customer and the firms which compete to serve him and offer him a free choice is one of the strongest elements of democracy.

There are also striking differences in the ways that the three sectors are financed. In the parliamentary sector, money comes mainly from taxes. In the club sector, it comes mainly from members' subscriptions and from voluntary givings. In the market sector, it comes mainly from customers.

A civil servant or local-government officer does not need to be motivated by money. Perhaps it is better if he is not, although a sense of frugality in the spending of other people's money could be useful. He is carrying out the common wishes of the people as expressed through parliament or local council. He does not have to know what people want, but rather to administer fairly what has already been decided.

The head of a professional or trade association or a charity needs to be reasonably well motivated by money, otherwise the organisation may die for lack of funds, but the raising of money is quite often secondary to some other purpose which is already accepted by its members.

A managing director in the market sector must seek out for himself the wishes of his customers and justify his firm's existence through its ability to sell. He is likely to have competitors who are selling similar goods or services to the same customers. His motivation to beat the competition and get business from the customers must be strong.

The continued existence of a firm depends on attracting more than enough money to cover expenses. Nobody is likely to want to do this unless he is keen to possess money. So, financial motivation is paramount in a managing director. Unless it is strong, he is unlikely to do a good job of serving the community.

The term 'community service' has come to have a special meaning, usually involving voluntary service towards helping the less fortunate. However, as we have seen, each of the three sectors of democracy provides its own kind of service. One may argue that it is as much a service to the community to work in the market sector and to serve able-bodied people who pay for what they receive, as it is to work in the Civil Service or a charity and to serve the less fortunate who cannot pay for what they receive. Indeed, the taxes paid by the able-bodied in the market sector are the main support for the needs of the less fortunate.

Finally, it is the author's experience that financial motivation is an important factor in upholding the ethical standards of a nation. Although there is a small amount of fraud going on all the time, by and large business firms have to be scrupulously honest in their transactions, otherwise they would not keep their customers, their employees and their suppliers. As Dr Samuel Johnson said, 'there are few ways in which a man is more innocently employed than in getting money'.

3

Planner or Persuader?

The French revolutionary leader, Robespierre, summed up leadership perhaps best of all. He said that 'a leader has two characteristics: he knows where he is going and he is able to persuade people to go with him.' This suggests that a leader should ideally be both a planner and a persuader. Sometimes it is possible for him to be successful in spite of being short of one of these skills. In this case, he must be able to use the skills of his top team to make up for any deficiency in his own abilities.

It has long been accepted that people may be broadly divided according to two types of personality: introvert and extrovert. This division has some similarities to recognition of the basic leadership skills of planning and persuading.

Some aspects of personality are now considered to be particular types of intelligence. In this chapter we will look at the leadership skills of planning and persuading as possibly two forms of intelligence which can, to some extent, be developed by training. With the word 'planning' we will associate the term 'conceptual skill'; with the word 'persuading' we will associate the term 'responsive skill'. As we shall see in due course, both these skills are possibly more important to a managing director, because he exercises leadership in the market sector, than to a leader in any other sector.

Conceptual skill can be used to make a contribution to long-

14

term leadership through the making of plans and designs and the thinking out of objectives. By contrast, responsive skill can be used to make a contribution to short-term, everyday leadership, for which persuading is particularly important. This last statement may seem surprising, for surely someone who responds is a follower, not a persuader? Surely his response follows from the stimulus of another person?

In fact, however, someone who responds quickly and effectively to other people is likely to have the capacity to become a leader of the short-term situation. As we used to say, he has the capacity to become a strong personality. He is the sort of person who is likely to learn the habit of imposing obligations on other people.

This habit of getting people to do things for him seems to arise from the fact that when, early in life, a person finds that he responds well to other people, he generally goes on to learn how to get them to respond to him. This is the logical next step in a mutually responsive situation. An example of it can be seen in the behaviour of animal-lovers towards their pets. The person who responds well to animals automatically goes on to learn how to make them respond to him. Hence he learns how to train them to do what he requires. He becomes a natural leader of his pet animals in the short-term situation. Likewise, the highly responsive person learns to require things of other people and hence to lead them in the immediate, short-term situation.

A managing director with good all-round leadership ability must be able to mix his responsive skill with a due measure of the conceptual skill necessary to lead his team in the longer-term situation. Most people have a mixture of both responsive and conceptual skills, but childhood influences and other factors may have caused them to develop one of these skills much more than the other.

Anyone who wishes to play a full part in the leadership of a working team needs to develop both types of skill and to pay particular attention to the type which is less developed.

Before this can be done, he must be able to recognise which type is less developed.

As an aid to recognition, we list below in Figure 1 the possible characteristics of people who are highly conceptual but whose responsive skill is weak. We also list the possible characteristics of people who are highly responsive but whose conceptual skill is weak. Although relatively few people are highly developed in one skill and extremely weak in the other, strong contrasts in the description of characteristics are useful in a recognition test.

Figure 1
CONTRASTS IN CONCEPTUAL AND RESPONSIVE SKILLS

Highly Conceptual	*Highly Responsive*
1 He knows where he is going but is less sure of the immediate tactics for getting there.	1 He is confident of his immediate tactics but is less sure of his ultimate goal.
2 He is slow to learn practical tasks unless given the logical reasoning behind them.	2 He is quick to learn practical tasks and is not greatly concerned with the logical reasoning behind them.
3 He enjoys solo work more than team work.	3 He enjoys team work more than solo work.
4 Information is more readily absorbed by him in logical sequence and annoyance is created if the logic of the sequence is broken or interrupted.	4 Information is more readily absorbed by him at random, in instant patterns, so the disturbance of a logical sequence is not annoying—it may be a welcome relief to boredom.
5 He has a good memory for the kind of logical sequences of facts given out in formal education.	5 He has a good memory for patterns of information, such as facial expressions. He is considered a good judge of character.

16

Highly Conceptual	*Highly Responsive*
6 He has a tendency to go on and on when putting across a point and equally a tendency to let the other person do so, for fear of missing something.	6 He has a tendency to make short points and expect an instant response, and equally a tendency to interrupt others and answer points before they have even been fully made.
7 He expects too much automatic action from others in a crisis.	7 He is automatically demanding of others in a crisis.
8 He is less likely to want the dominant position in a hierarchy, although he may end up near the top—like the archbishop in relation to the medieval king.	8 He is more likely to want the dominant position in a hierarchy, although as 'king' he may crave the support of an 'archbishop'.
9 His tendency to conceptuality is self-reinforcing. Early habits of logical thinking, if well developed, can make it harder to keep up with the bombardment of signals around him, until he becomes an 'absent-minded professor'.	9 His tendency to responsiveness is self-reinforcing. Early habits of quick response, if well developed, make it harder for him to follow patiently a logical sequence of information and he is easily distracted by the bombardment of signals from people around him, until he finds it difficult to learn new ideas and grasp new concepts.
10 If he is inclined to be selfish, it will be in the longer-term. As he is not so good at getting his own way in immediate, short-term encounters, he schemes for longer-term goals and hopes to sneak up on the outside to score. If generous-hearted, he will give away much in the short-term provided he can feel he is adhering to longer-term goals.	10 If he is inclined to be selfish, it will be in the short-term. He is good at winning in immediate, short-term encounters and so he expects to win. He will want at least a minor concession to his point of view even when he must concede the major point. If generous-hearted, he will give away much in the long-term provided he is allowed immediate victories.

17

Highly Conceptual	*Highly Responsive*
11 He says what he means during a negotiation even if this makes him 'wooden'.	11 He says things he does not mean during a negotiation in order to obtain some kind of response and weigh up the position.
12 He thinks automatically of doing things himself rather than of getting other people to do them.	12 He thinks automatically of requiring other people to do things rather than doing them himself.
13 He is good at intellectual discussion, which helps him to see the broad picture, but he is poor at 'small talk' and hence he tends to silence when small talk is required.	13 He is good at 'small talk', which helps him to get to know people, but he is poor at intellectual discussion and hence he tends to use break-up tactics when such discussion begins.
14 He is poor at committee work but good at individual, imaginative planning.	14 He is good at committee work and likes 'group thinking' in which several people contribute to an idea. His planning is realistic rather than imaginative.
15 He was possibly bullied when a boy.	15 He was possibly the bully when a boy.
16 He tends to ignore the need for good personal relationships but if he worries about them he is meticulous, almost to the point of being over-fussy about people.	16 He takes personal relationships as a matter of course and carries them off with an easy confidence.
17 He takes planning for granted and carries if off with an easy confidence.	17 He tends to ignore planning but if he worries about it he is meticulous, almost to the point of being over-fussy about detail.
18 He wants to get his ideas across.	18 He wants to be leader of the day to day situation.

18

Highly Conceptual	Highly Responsive
19 He consciously or subconsciously experiments with ideas.	19 He consciously or subconsciously experiments in the manipulation of people.
20 He subconsciously expects other people to follow a logical sequence of information.	20 He is ever conscious of the severe limits to human attention and is closely observant of signs of boredom.
21 He expects the information he conveys to be exciting to others, in its own right.	21 He often creates 'cliff-hangers' to make people curious about the information he is about to convey. They may be very simple, such as: 'I have two objections to that'.
22 He can write a good report but will probably make only an average presentation of it to the management committee or client.	22 His report-writing is average but his presentation to the management committee or client is more likely to be convincing.
23 He quickly grasps the overall new theme of a speech or paper but he may miss any danger signals for his present organisation and its activities.	23 He may miss the overall new theme of a speech or paper but he quickly notices any danger signals for his present organisation and its activities.
24 He likes going to parties if they provide an opportunity for searching intellectual discussion with one or two people.	24 He likes going to parties if they provide an opportunity for many brief encounters.
25 He may fail to reply immediately to a convincing statement because he wants to think it over.	25 He is likely to reply immediately to a convincing statement with sceptical questions or even hostile rebuttals.
26 His natural inclination in the handling of a negotiation is to circulate a detailed paper on what he thinks should be agreed	26 His natural inclination in the handling of a negotiation is first to circulate a suggested agenda of topics which he thinks need

Highly Conceptual | *Highly Responsive*

and then, usually in vain, to try to persuade the other parties to agree, all in one meeting.

discussion and to invite additions, then to hold a preliminary meeting at which the easiest items are agreed, circulate the minutes setting out what has been agreed and what remains for settlement, and finally to hold another meeting to discuss the basics.

27 He is inclined to be religious in the sense of being governed by the concepts of a 'whole-life' creed such as Christianity, or a 'work-place' creed such as scientific method, engineering design or business planning.

27 He is inclined to be bored by religion but excited by manipulative techniques, such as sport, amateur dramatics, selling, buying and contract negotiation.

28 His motivations are primarily long-term, stemming from the logical sequences of concepts which build up in his mind. If B follows from A, and C is the logical next step, then this is his goal.

28 His motivations are primarily short-term, stemming from the habits he has developed of getting people to react to him and do things for him. He feels his way along from one reaction to the next.

29 He is likely to be better at names.

29 He is likely to be better at faces.

30 He is capable of making the great conceptual leaps which, on a rare occasion, will produce a best-selling product and a fortune, but which are more likely to produce losses through being way ahead of the customers. He is generally considered to be a bad businessman unless working closely with a responsive colleague.

30 He is responsive to the gradual changes in customer attitudes which are so important if a firm's products or services are to stay in demand. He is generally considered to be a reliable businessman who never goes too far out in front, but he can be floored by a major shift in his market unless he works closely with a conceptual colleague.

4

The Well-Rounded Manager

Most business leaders have a good balance of conceptual and responsive skills, but they are likely to be employing people who are weak on one side or the other and whose full potential cannot be realised until they are encouraged and aided in improving the weaker skill. It is generally possible to bring about an improvement by training. This chapter gives some indication of what can be done.

Conceptual Skill
Almost everyone has some capacity for thinking about the future, making plans and conceiving new ideas. If a person is determined to make the most of this capacity, he may be surprised to find that it is larger than he had thought. As Thomas Edison said, 'Genius is ten per cent inspiration and ninety per cent perspiration.' If one just gets on with the job of perspiring, maybe the ideas will come.

There are broadly three ways of making full use of one's conceptual capacity. The first is to discipline the process by which one thinks ahead and plans future activity. This process is mostly conducted with the aid of diaries, work schedules and budgets.

We cannot discuss budgeting in this chapter, because it comes later in the book. Nor can we discuss here the specific types of work scheduling which middle management needs to

21

Monday	Tuesday	Wednesday	Thursday	Friday	Sat/Sun
6 June Start xyz Report	7 June	8 June Revise second half-year budgets	9 June	10 June	11/12 June
13 June	14 June	15 June	16 June	17 June	18/19 June
20 June	21 June	22 June	23 June Circulate xyz Report to Board	24 June Revised budgets to management committee	25/26 June
27 June	28 June	29 June	30 June	1 July	2/3 July

Figure 2 Work sheet

operate, on a team basis, for the progressing of customers' orders. What we can do here is to discuss the use of diaries and work sheets by top management to ensure that personal work schedules are maintained, that tasks are given the right priority and that they are completed on time.

Figure 2 illustrates a personal work schedule in which dates are set out in side by side columns. The starts of tasks are entered on a shaded background and completions are entered on a clear background The advantage of this method of layout is that it uses a convention which is now quite widely accepted in Europe, as we shall see in Chapter 8—that information which is definite should have a clear background and be made quite distinct from information which is more vague.

Figure 2 illustrates the use of this convention. Suppose a managing director undertakes to circulate a report to the board on 16 June. He should enter this commitment on the clear background section of the form for this date. If he estimates that the report will take ten days to prepare he should note the need to start preparation of the report on 6 June. This, however, should be entered on a shaded background, because the report could be started on 5 June if time was available then, or it might be possible to postpone the start until 7 June if 6 June proved to be a particularly busy day.

Every morning the managing director should look at his work schedule and note the tasks which ought to be started, although none of these may be urgent, and also the tasks which must urgently be completed. By keeping the 'oughts' separate from the 'musts', he is disciplining his mind to be continually ticking over on the problems associated with the former at the same time as he takes care not to overlook deadlines for the latter.

It is possible, as Figure 3 shows, to keep a combined diary and work schedule. The projected starting dates of tasks are entered on a shaded background but the completions and appointments are both entered on clear. An advantage of

Monday	Tuesday	Wednesday	Thursday	Friday	Sat/Sun
6 June	7 June	8 June	9 June	10 June	11/12 June
		Revise second half-year budgets			
10 am Brown 4 pm Jones	Lunch Smith	11 am Robinson	7.50 am St Pancras VISIT SHEFFIELD BRANCH	9 am Thompson 10 am Jackson 11 am Robson 2 pm Smithson 3 pm Clarkson 4 pm Timson	
13 June	14 June	15 June	16 June	17 June	18/19 June
			Circulate XYZ Report to Board	Revised budgets to management committee	
------- TRADE FAIR -------			2 pm Hammond	11 am Cameron	

Figure 3 Combined diary and work schedule

keeping a combined work schedule and diary is that any clash between the completion date for a major task and a time-consuming series of appointments is immediately obvious.

The second way to make full use of conceptual capacity is to ensure that there are quiet periods when one's biological computer, or brain, can process the information it has absorbed and 'print it out'. The brain can do some of this processing during the night, but if one is never quiet by day, there is limited opportunity to listen for the answers to problems.

The traditional word for a quiet time, honoured over the centuries, is prayer. The nearest modern equivalent is a five-word phrase: 'Switch off that damned radio'.

Quiet periods are essential at the office in order to write the reports, get the plans down on paper, and so forth, but there is a saying that 'the office is no place to work'. It can be a good place to communicate with colleagues, but too much communication leaves very little quiet time.

A basic rule in office layout is never to have more than two people in the same work area. The old adage, 'two's company, three's a crowd', is worthy of great respect. When two people occupy the same area, one is likely to be away some of the time. When he is not, at least he cannot easily start a conversation if the other person wants to be quiet. If three people occupy the same area, the chance of any of them enjoying quietness is greatly reduced.

The problem of achieving quietness for planning and conceptual work is so serious that some companies have experimented with a universal quiet time. All managers are expected to come in early but not to meet together, use the telephone or open the mail. In research laboratories this problem has sometimes been tackled by providing special quiet rooms. For example, at the big General Electric laboratories at Schenectady, New York, there are quiet rooms off the library where a scientist who has completed an experiment can retire to write up his results. In Britain, a widely used practice for achieving quiet time is to stay at home for the day. This only emphasises the need for better office design.

Finally, it is advisable to make the most of the best quiet period of the day—in bed. When one shares a room with a spouse, the bedside lighting has to be subtle, but older people with management responsibilities sometimes have separate rooms. They need to be able to make notes about problems and their possible solutions whenever they wake in the night. They generally ignore the old-fashioned advice that you should go to bed and not worry about your work, for they find that sleep comes more easily after making notes on a problem and thereby increasing one's understanding of it. The computer then churns away during sleep and, with any luck, it may come up with an answer in the morning.

The third way to make full use of one's conceptual capacity is to aid the brain in its task of absorbing, classifying and recalling information. Many people complain that they have a bad memory or that they cannot recall facts when needed. If this is true, they are obviously handicapped in their ability to plan well or to conceive a new product. Planning and creative work involves the ability to recall pieces of information which at first sight may seem unconnected but which actually fit together into the 'jigsaw' of the new plan or idea.

Some people are clearly better than others at the recall of associated facts, but however good they are, they cannot recall facts which were not actually recorded in the brain. When a person complains that he cannot recall a particular fact, very often his problem is that he did not actually take it in. At most times of the day, to get a message stored in the brain when so much else is going on around is no mean feat.

A well-tried method of improving the flow of key information into the brain is to keep repeating it and to ensure that some of these repetitions occur when there are no distractions. One way of providing opportunity to repeat key pieces of information is to maintain a recording diary. This need not be a separate book from one's appointments diary.

A recording diary should be entered up fully in the evening if there is no other time, but brief reminder notes should be made during the course of the day. Evening is also a good time to review the entries, some of which may be concerned with problems and some with solutions. By turning back the pages and re-reading the items, one is reinforcing the impact of each item on the mind and thus motivating it to proceed with solving some of the problems.

A more sophisticated version of this method involves the use of pocket-size index cards. Each separate idea, fact or problem is entered on a separate card as soon as convenient after it arises. At the end of the day or when travelling on a train or 'plane, the card entries can be reviewed and the cards sorted into appropriate groups. Rubber bands can be used to secure separate groups of cards. The very act of sorting and re-reading the cards strengthens the mind's ability to absorb key information and classify it, so that these facts are ready for recall. The cards prepared on any subject are also an invaluable aid to planning and report writing, etc. They can be re-sorted and laid out in any suitable order, ready for drafting a plan or report, or for preparing a presentation or speech.

Responsive Skill

The time-honoured method of learning how to persuade is to learn how to sell. Many a businessman has confided to the author that the episode in his life which first made him sit up and begin to understand what a difficult art persuasion can be, was when he first went on the road selling the firm's products.

Anyone who desperately needs to come away from a customer with an order, if he is going to keep his job, learns to grow up very fast. He begins to observe customer reactions which had previously gone unnoticed. He learns to discard conversation ploys which do not work or which produce an undesired effect. He starts remembering, for repeat use, those statements and questions which produce a positive response.

One of the turning points in the author's career came when he heard a successful businessman say: 'Doers are two a penny. It is good sellers who are rare'. This statement is largely true, but it seemed at the time a shocking commentary on a world which is short of good 'doers' who can design and produce really worthwhile and flawless products. The modern emphasis on marketing, and the high rewards which it offers to those few who are really good at it, must surely be due, in part, to the neglect of marketing and salesmanship by the public education system.

When over three-quarters of the working population are employed in the market sector, it seems odd that the education system should almost entirely neglect to teach salesmanship. One can hardly expect the general quality of products to be high if selling skill is so rare that those who possess it can make a good living by selling rubbish.

Salesmanship is a well documented and disciplined skill which is basic to the art of persuasion as practised in government and the voluntary associations as well as in industry. It is a skill which can be acquired, up to a fair level of competence, by a substantial proportion of the population.

There are many books on salesmanship and these make a good beginning, but a practical course in selling is even better. Sales training also needs continual reinforcement, particularly for those who do not already have a high degree of responsive skill. For this purpose a sales newsletter can be helpful.

The author did not learn to sell until he was over fifty years old and then he learnt it with no difficulty from the English-language version of the European-wide fortnightly newsletter for salesmen, *Sales Force Info*. This extraordinary newsletter has been so successful that it appears in eight languages. It has the advantage that it reads like a newspaper, even though it is teaching old tricks to new dogs.

The logic behind the art of persuasion can be seen if one studies all the various ways in which a highly responsive person uses questions and statements in order to persuade, and then compares them with the quite different ways in which questions and statements are generally used by a person with poor responsive skill. We give in Figure 4 a comparison of this kind, with examples.

Figure 4 is of curiosity value to those who already have highly developed responsive skill. They know how to do, superbly well, the sort of verbal tricks with questions and statements which are illustrated. Figure 4 is chiefly of value to those who obtained very good examination results at school and university but were not great sportsmen or participators in student activities.

The education system inevitably concentrates on using questions for seeking information and statements for giving facts. The 'natural swots' among students are inclined to remain immature because they naively assume that other people in the outside world are doing the same thing. They can fall into this trap with particular ease because in their long years of study they are continually mixing with others who live and work by the same simple assumption. They are usually confined to an educational atmosphere for some twenty years, from about the age of five to twenty-five, and nobody can deny that these are formative years. It is rather like caging a lion for the equivalent period of its life in a zoo where all bodily requirements are met and the lion can only walk up and down the one path facing the spectators. His ability at hunting in the competitive world outside is bound to be affected.

The long period of scholastic cloisterhood in which many of the most able young people become emmeshed today is part of the reason why sons of businessmen so often find it difficult to follow their fathers into the family business—particularly if father is a self-made man. The son learns at college to treat a statement of fact for what it is, but if in doubt, to question it. Then he goes home and is bewildered to find his father using combinations of words which are not aimed at

29

telling him anything or even asking him something. Their purpose is to persuade him to courses of action that he has not had time to think through. As a consequence he resents the whole persuasive approach to life and he either declines to go into the business or, if he agrees, becomes a weak leader who is poor at marketing and at industrial relations.

Fortunately the situation is not beyond redemption. This same well educated young person has the habit of learning. Once he is enabled to realise that there is a logic to persuasion and that it can be learnt like any other discipline, he can usually become extraordinarily good at it.

Figure 4
THE LOGIC OF PERSUASION AS ILLUSTRATED BY CONTRASTS BETWEEN THE WAYS IN WHICH QUESTIONS AND STATEMENTS ARE USED BY PERSONS WITH LOW AND HIGH LEVELS OF RESPONSIVE SKILL

Low Responsive Skill	*High Responsive Skill*
1 Use of	Questions
People with low responsive skill use questions almost solely to seek information.	Highly responsive people use questions for a large number of purposes:
Example: 'How many people are coming?'	1 To seek information. *Example:* 'How many people are coming?' 2 To assess attitudes. *Example:* 'Do you really want to come?' 3 To break in on a discussion. *Example:* 'But is that fair to those who come? 4 To throw doubt on a proposed course of action and seek a reconsideration. *Example:* 'Do you think it is right for them to come all this way on the day before the conference?'

30

Low Responsive Skill　　　　　　*High Responsive Skill*

5 To obtain reassurance of another's performance.
Example: 'Are you quite certain you can arrive in time for the opening?'
6 To obtain action from someone without giving an instruction.
Example: 'Don't you think you ought to come too?'

2 Use of Statements

People with poor responsive skill use statements of fact almost solely in order to give information to others.

Example: 'About forty-five people are coming.'

Highly responsive people use statements of fact for a variety of purposes:

1 To give information.
Example: 'About forty-five people are coming.'
2 To provoke someone into revealing facts or attitudes.
Example: 'You won't get more than about thirty people coming.'
3 To obtain reactions to a proposed course.
Example: 'If there is not enough happening, I may suggest that they do not come.'
4 To make a veiled threat, in order to seek reconsideration of a policy.
Example: 'If that plan is adopted we will have nobody coming from the south.'
5 To announce an intention and challenge the boss to dare to disagree, at the same time making it clear that there is no intention of seeking formal approval.
Example: 'I'm planning to grant a special allowance to those in my division who come.'

31

Low Responsive Skill	*High Responsive Skill*

3 Use of Statements plus Questions

People with poor responsive skill use statements plus questions almost solely to check their own knowledge.	Highly responsive people use statements plus questions for a variety of purposes:
Example: 'Let me repeat it. We turn right at the cross-roads and then take the second on the left. Is that correct?'	1 To seek a definite commitment to a desired course of action. *Example:* 'You are coming, aren't you?' 2 To press for acceptance of an intended action. *Example:* 'I don't need to come, do I?' 3 To finalise an agreement. *Example:* 'I suggest that the northern and eastern divisions come this time and the southern and western divisions next time. That would be fair, don't you think?' 4 To obtain agreement to a proposed course of action. *Example:* 'I could bring the van if I come. What do you think?' 5 To disguise a request for permission in the form of a co-operative statement. *Example:* 'I propose to come a day before the official start. If I do, can I give you a hand in getting ready?'

The logic of persuasion is concerned with leading people towards the course of action proposed by the persuader, helping them to reach their own decision in favour of this course. It is basically the same logic, whether one is selling to a customer, presenting a plan to top management or persuading employees to co-operate in an unusual assignment.

32

Selling is a particular form of logic which involves playing the statement and question game until you strike the customer on his raw nerve. When you know what he really wants and can show him that you can supply it, you are close to winning.

It is difficult for the managing director who has always had a high level of responsive skill to realise why many members of his working team, who are highly competent at their technology but lack responsive skill, fail to put their point of view across. If these people were encouraged and aided in learning salesmanship and were given opportunity to try their hand at selling, some would undoubtedly rush back to the cocoon of their technology; others would have their eyes opened to new prospects of developing their ability to persuade and thereby make the most of their technical skill. There can also be a valuable feedback from this kind of exercise. When a technologist comes face to face with customers, his creative abilities are usually strengthened by first-hand information on what is really wanted. In this way, he becomes a better technologist.

5

Discerning Market Trends

Why do some people succeed in business in spite of doing rather badly at school? Why are the super-intelligent sometimes out of place in business? Answers to both these questions may lie in the findings of Dr Robert Ornstein of the Langley-Porter Neuropsychiatric Institute of California, first reported in 1974.

Dr Ornstein's researches brought him to the conclusion that the education system has in the past been wasting, or leaving untrained, half of human brain-power. Our brains have two hemispheres, a left and a right. The left hemisphere, according to Ornstein's findings, handles our ability with words and other skills used in the education system. The right hemisphere has spatial skills and others which are largely unused at school, including artistic talent and intuitive processes not yet well understood, and this is the half which Dr Ornstein believes is being wasted.

Some of the key skills needed by a managing director possibly lie in this right hemisphere of the brain. Generally, to be successful he must be more a co-ordinator of other people's talents than a specialist in one talent himself. He must know how to find the people, the information and the resources to produce and market a product or service which people actually want to buy.

There is, however, more to it than this. The businessman

who comes up with a winning idea is generally obsessed with a vision, a truth which he cannot prove—except by trying it on the customer. The process which he must carry out before winning the full approval of a large number of customers is rather different from the research methods used by academics. A different part of the brain may well be used for these two activities and, in this case, a rigorous system of training in research methods would tend to inhibit the development of those skills needed in business for discerning market trends.

The pattern of business activity is continually changing in response to an on-going series of transactions between buyers and sellers. Both parties are only trying to do the best possible deal for themselves, but the consequence of a large number of people trying to do this is that they are all being edged along by the hidden hand of market forces, in directions which none of them individually planned to pursue. This is a natural result of individuals exercising free choice.

Every market has trends which, if discerned correctly, can lead to fortune, and if ignored or misjudged, can lead to bankruptcy. What are the qualities needed in a managing director if he is to have a better than average chance of discerning correctly the trends in the market for his particular goods or services? There is no easy answer to this question, for disciplined research on it has been scanty. The author can hardly do more than make his contribution to the debate by taking a further step in discussion of the leadership skills which were the subject of the last two chapters.

These two skills are probably needed in rather similar proportions for discerning market trends. A leaning one way or the other could be a serious handicap. On the one hand, the person who looks for generalisations to fit every set of data could find that working in business was like building a house on shifting sand. Equally, the person who responds very well to the everyday situation but is not prepared to make a serious study of the data available to him, is not likely to discern many market trends.

35

What seems to be needed in business is a capacity for continual interplay between conceptual and responsive skills. The interplay involves continually responding, like any good salesman, to the behaviour of customers from day to day, meeting their needs as well as possible and meanwhile storing their reactions and attitudes in the brain for use in building new concepts of what the market wants.

These new concepts can rarely be put to rigorous test before committing the company to large expenditure on preparing to launch a new or modified product. Market research is limited in what it can tell the businessman. Its simplest and most reliable role is to measure the overall size of the market. For example, a managing director could hardly go on thinking that his firm might sell 3 million men's hats a year after the researchers had estimated, from sample interviews, that there were only 2 million men who were likely to wear a hat.

What market research cannot do with enough precision is to gather useful opinions on a proposed new product. This situation is too hypothetical. Even if the new product is actually produced in small numbers and shown to potential customers, their answers to a question on whether they would buy it are not generally very meaningful.

It is of more value to test part of the market by making the product available in one area through the normal channels of distribution, advertising it in this area and finding out whether people do actually buy it. Test marketing is, however, expensive and, by the time a company is ready to undertake it, they are heavily committed to many aspects of a full launching. The product has already been developed, production facilities have been created and a small quantity of the product has been manufactured.

A managing director cannot ever hope, therefore, to run his business on a completely tidy, pre-planned basis, There may never be a clear-cut situation where he can develop new or modified products, research their markets, plan their launchings and expect everything to go just right. His mental processes need to be as disciplined as those of a scientific researcher, but his tactics need to be very flexible and a change of course may sometimes become extremely urgent. The general pattern of his work is likely to run somewhat along the following lines:

He must get personally involved in the detail of product development and marketing, keep asking questions and probing for reactions. He must resist the temptation to seek a generalisation in every set of data, yet his conceptual skill must be sufficiently well developed for him to wake up sometimes in the night and realise new truths about the nature of his market. He must not allow himself to become too enthusiastic about such distillations of wisdom, yet he must seek every opportunity to test them out at minimum cost to the company.

Trial and error is the old-fashioned expression which comes nearest to describing the continuing interplay of conceptuality and responsiveness which is needed in a businessman who wants to have a better than average chance of correctly discerning market trends. If he knows from his own background experience that his abilities in these two respects are not well balanced, one of the most convenient ways to achieve a balance lies in the company chairmanship. Every managing director needs a confidant with whom he can have close and frequent business discussions, and the most convenient confidant is the chairman.

If the MD happens to be a highly responsive person who is good at handling day to day problems with customers, employees and suppliers, then he is likely to benefit from working with a highly conceptual chairman who thinks more deeply about long-term trends. Equally, if the MD happens to be a highly conceptual person who has perhaps won his spurs by the clever design of a new product range or the opening up of a new approach to marketing, then he is likely to benefit from working with a highly responsive chairman who notices any little tell-tale signs of impending trouble and who presents a more extrovert image to employees, customers and the public.

Now that we have examined the typical interplay between conceptual and responsive skills which business management needs if it is to have a better than average chance of discerning market trends, we can put flesh on the bare bones by presenting some vignettes of the ever-changing market scene which a managing director must endeavour to understand.

What Marks & Spencer Ltd did to Manufacturing

Once upon a time manufacturers had their own salesmen knocking on the doors of wholesalers and retailers, selling the goods which their own staff had designed. This still happens in many industries, but only to a limited extent, for Marks & Spencer Ltd developed and turned the tables on their own suppliers. Instead of sitting in their offices waiting for manufacturers to show them what they had to offer, M & S executives went to the factories and told their suppliers what to make. Even though M & S were retailers, they did their own market research and their own product design and materials research, so they were able, in many ways, to decide exactly what to specify to their suppliers.

They went even further. Every aspect of the production process might be discussed with the supplier and, if necessary, he was given advice on how he could improve the efficiency of his production, and also how to operate effective costing and control methods. Then a production contract was arranged which specified long, uninterrupted production runs which therefore kept the costs down, but which did not involve warehousing expenses. Delivery schedules were arranged requiring the regular dispatch of goods direct from the factory to the M & S retail branches.

This system has been accompanied by rigorous inspection of products and processes. The M & S inspectors rarely announce their visit to a supplier—particularly a food supplier. He has to run his business in first-class condition at all times, for fear that the inspectors might suddenly appear.

The M & S methods of purchasing goods for their shops have been a boon to the stores' customers and have given it virtually worldwide acclaim. What they have done for manufacturers who had come to depend on their contracts is another story. To be left high and dry without a renewal of a long-run contract can lead to financial ruin. Suppliers have had to learn to be wary of becoming over-dependent on M & S.

If this system of purchasing was carried to its logical conclusion, large sectors of manufacturing industry would become mere order-fillers, completely dependent on the marketing skills of the High Street stores. Inventive genius among suppliers could be stifled. Fortunately, the revolution in retailing has not gone that far. M & S do not, in fact, plan all their requirements in advance—far from it. Manufacturers still beat a path to their door to show them what they have designed and developed on their own initiative, hoping to win a long-run production contract if the first trial order proves satisfactory.

Nevertheless, M & S pioneered a shift in the centre of business initiative, away from manufacturing and into the buying departments of the chain stores. This is a shift which no managing director can afford to ignore.

What Nationalisation of Steel did to Stockholding

Nationalisation of the steel-producing industry in Britain gave a near-total monopoly of home-based supply to one company which was, however, subject to competition from imports. This semi-monopolistic position would be likely to blunt the competitive marketing edge of the British steel-producing industry. Absence of personal ownership in the industry could blunt it even further.

If every user of steel had to buy direct from the steel mills, his business could be seriously handicapped by long delays between placing an order and waiting for a batch of the right kind and section of steel to be rolled for his needs. The risk that steel users might have their work held up by a temporary shortage of a special steel has led to the growth of privately owned steel stockholders who know their customers' requirements and who can generally be relied upon to meet most needs quickly. They also know where to buy the right steel abroad if they cannot obtain it from the monopolistic home industry. So steel stockholding has become big business. It offers scope for initiative to some of the sharpest business brains and provides an important service to customers who would otherwise be at the mercy of one supplier.

What the Wrapping did to Bread

Sliced and wrapped bread became big business after World War II. The fact that wrapped bread stayed fresh longer meant that a large bakery with modern equipment could produce bread at low cost and sell it over a wide area served by a fleet of delivery vans. Faced with this new type of competition, many small, old-fashioned bakeries went into liquidation.

Wrapped bread, however, is not to everybody's taste. In due course, the demand for 'home-baked' bread revived and, with it, the opportunity for small bakeries and small chains of bakers to meet the local demand for more distinct styles of loaf.

What the Airlines did to Hotels

The growth of air travel led to the rapid expansion of hotel chains which spanned the earth, offering the business traveller a reliable standard of service which was virtually the same in each major city. In due course, many experienced travellers became bored by the monotony of the service and facilities. Hence, there was a revival in the fortunes of the 'country house' type of hotel, offering a more individual and unusual service.

What the Shopping Precinct did to the Specialist Shop

The building of new shopping centres and the turning of High Streets into traffic-free areas have generally led to an increase in rents which some of the more individualist and specialist shops could not afford. Consequently, they have had to close down or move out. The new precinct depends for its success on attracting the major chain stores which tend to attract more business if they are near each other. When enough chain stores join a precinct, it can be a great success. If, however, one of the major chains carries out very thorough market research on the catchment areas of a new shopping development and concludes that it will not pay to establish itself there, the decision of this store to stay out can seal the fate of the whole development.

Some of the big chain stores operate on such a scale that they will not go into a town or a shopping centre unless it is almost certain to attract a very large volume of business. This means that some of the smaller towns can never attract the big chains. So, it is generally possible to distinguish between those shopping centres which have all the big chains and have become mass shopping areas, and the quieter, smaller town centres which have become refuges for the more individualist and specialist shops and their customers.

What Work Stoppages did for Dual Sourcing

The trend towards large-scale production facilities operating at a high level of efficiency has been brought up against the harsh reality that big organisations are less personal for individual workers. Industrial relations in large establishments are generally worse than in smaller ones, as has been shown by Department of Employment statistics.

If production is concentrated in one major plant of a company and industrial relations break down, a strike can put the firm's customers in jeopardy by cutting off their supplies—hence the rise of dual sourcing. The customer insists on production being split between two factories which are

41

geographically far apart and which are therefore unlikely to involve similar industrial relations problems simultaneously. So, here is a constraint on manufacturers which must be taken into account in every plan for expansion of production facilities.

What the Garden Centre did to the Old Nursery

Among the old horticultural nurseries which were operating in Britain before 1960, the ones which had the best chance of survival were those which happened to be situated beside a busy road where weekend traffic would lead to a natural growth of custom from passing motorists. Without this increase in business arising from the growth in motoring population, there could be little prospect of expanding a horticultural nursery into a major garden centre selling tools, furniture, fertilisers and chemicals, indoor plants, swimming pools, etc, in addition to the usual small plants, shrubs and trees.

What happened to those nurseries which were not so fortunate as to be well located for the steady expansion of their general business? Many went bankrupt, but some survived by specialising in the large-scale production of a limited range of plants which happened to be particularly well suited to their area. These plants were wholesaled to garden centres all over the country.

Thus, the garden centres steadily adapted themselves to producing less and less of what they sold, concentrating instead on stocking a very wide range of plants, equipment and supplies.

The changing trends illustrated by the preceding seven examples are all fairly obvious when they are put down on paper. Yet they might each be extremely difficult to see and understand if one was actually engaged in a particular trade which was undergoing a change of this kind. The day to day problems and the personal involvement in a business make it very hard to see the wood for the trees. Nevertheless, the attempt must be made and we have suggested that a managing director generally needs to be both highly conceptual and very responsive if he is to have a better than average chance of discerning market trends.

6

Co-ordinating the Tasks

THERE IS A TIME AND PLACE FOR DECISIONS

Should a managing director make all the major decisions of the business on his own, or should he encourage a high degree of participation by other members of his working team? It seems obvious today that he should encourage participation, yet personal decision-makers have had a vogue among the management pundits. The 1960s saw the rise of the cult of decision-making, where the stature of an executive was measured by the decisions he took. This was even carried to the absurdity of evaluating the pay for a management job in terms of the number and types of decisions made and how long a decision might stand before its maker was found out if it went wrong.

Fortunately, when something is carried to absurdity its weaknesses are quickly exposed. So, when managers tried to measure decisions for the purpose of putting a value on a job, they came up against the stark fact that very few decisions should be made in isolation by a single executive, even by the managing director. Indeed, the badly run firms are usually those in which far too many solus decisions are made.

In such firms, most people affected by a decision do not even hear about it until rather late in the day. Someone has gone to the boss and obtained a spontaneous decision. The very way in which it was made means that many of the people who should have been involved in it were left out. When a middle manager complains of communication being bad in his firm, he usually means that too many decisions are made at the top without consulting those affected by them.

What is the right time and place for a managing director to make decisions? Usually at a regular meeting of his main heads of departments. Preferably, he should hold frequent, brief meetings at a quiet time of the day or week. How often and when he holds them will depend on the nature of the business, but the more frequent the meetings, the less need to flout the system and make urgent decisions without a meeting.

Some of the problems which he is obliged to settle in a hurry may arise from the fact that his own employees have neglected to keep him abreast of events. To minimise the risk of being caught unawares, he should encourage his subordinates, by his questioning technique, to report fully and frankly about what has been happening and about what they are planning to do. Their reports should include emergency decisions which had to be taken instanteously, and also those which they expect to make and which need to be discussed in advance with the MD and colleagues, either to be confirmed or steered in a different direction. The managing director should likewise report to his departmental heads.

An operating management meeting should generally be chaired by the MD himself. His chief role as chairman of the meeting is to make or confirm decisions in the presence of his main heads of departments, after first hearing their views and discussing his own views with them.

A managing director is essentially a co-ordinator. He cannot leave decisions to a vote of the members of his operating committee because they are interested parties, ie, heads of the departments which need to be co-ordinated. He must make the decisions himself, but as far as possible make them in the presence of those affected.

Why so much emphasis on co-ordination? Because this is vital to organisations operating in the market sector. One cannot sell effectively to a customer unless care is taken over every aspect of the product or service—the materials used, the processes, the wrappings, the advertising, the delivery, the price, etc. Someone has to have a vision of what the total product or service should be like and, in most cases, this can only be the managing director. As co-ordinator, he is in a position to hear and see all aspects, so he must make the key decisions which affect those aspects.

In aircraft manufacture, for example, present technology requires that the aircraft should have both wings and an engine, or possibly more than one. Someone has to assume overall responsibility for seeing that the work of the wing-makers fits together with the work of the engine-makers to produce an aircraft which is both flyable as a technical product and viable as a commercial product.

It has been said that 'a camel is a horse designed by a committee'. If this is a fair assessment of the design of a camel, then it must be added that camel design could not have been the work of a properly conducted, operating management committee.

The logic of decision-making in an operating management committee is in line with that of the business organisaton itself. There has to be a managing director or equivalent at the top, with heads of various departments, such as sales, production and finance, reporting to him so that he co-ordinates their efforts. They in turn have various specialist functions reporting to them and so on down the hierarchy, as shown in Figure 5.

The managing director has, in fact, twin problems of co-ordination. He must co-ordinate all of today's activities within various parts of the business and he must co-ordinate today with tomorrow. An example of the latter is seen in the problem of expansion. To expand the business too fast today, just because there is currently a boom in demand for its products, could lead to running short of capital and even to bankruptcy. Equally, to cut down too savagely in a recession

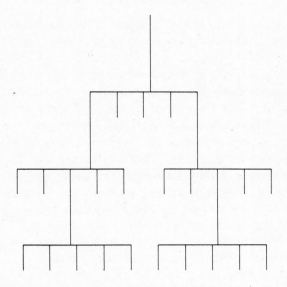

Figure 5 Typical co-ordinating management structure

could mean losing key employees who might not be available for recruitment again when the recession ends. The MD must act as continuity man between the past, present and future.

Authority in a business firm is ultimately derived from customer buying-power. If the customers do not buy, the firm dies. Therefore, authority must reside in the person at the top of the organisation, the managing director, who co-ordinates all efforts towards satisfying the customers.

The nature of authority is largely independent of whether the capital for the business is provided by private interests or from public funds. In both cases, the managing director can be sacked by the providers of capital, if he is not himself the owner of a majority of the company's voting shares. But, subject only to retaining his office, he carries the power of decision-making. Although he should consult his heads of departments so that his decisions are correct in relation to the products and the customers and fair in relation to the employees, he is nevertheless consulting them, not seeking

47

their approval. The decisions must, in the last resort, be his if the firm is to operate on the basis that everyone is pulling together.

The managing director who owns all or most of his company's shares does not have to answer to anyone for his decisions, although he may, as a matter of courtesy, keep any minority shareholders informed of the company's affairs. Many managing directors are, however, answerable to a formal board of directors. This is usually the case in the larger and older family businesses, in subsidiary companies, in public listed companies and firms owned by government. In such cases, the managing director does not generally make his day to day operating decisions in the presence of his board of directors. He makes these with his heads of departments, although some of them may be on the board.

The role of the board in relation to the managing director is quite different from that of the operating committee. As elected representatives of the shareholders, their main responsibilities are twofold. First, the board is continually and quietly evaluating the MD's stewardship. Is the company doing well and if not, is this the managing director's fault? The directors cannot easily participate in deciding the detail of policy, unless they happen to work in the business, but by their questions at board meetings they can endeavour to maintain a running assessment of the man in charge, in case a decision to replace him should ever be necessary.

Secondly, the board is concerned with budgets. They will want to approve both the operating budgets and the capital expenditure budgets. In discussing these the board will be concerned to look beyond the plans actually presented and consider whether they involve commitments which, once entered into, are not easily ended and which, if not ended, could become a bottomless pit into which money must be continually poured. If more capital is needed by the firm, the managing director will require the board's approval. It is not so difficult to discuss a well laid out plan for expansion which requires additional capital; the biggest problem for a board arises when the need for further capital sneaks up on them due to plans going awry or commitments arising which had not been fully foreseen.

In most companies, the managing director must be forever facing both ways. He must face towards his board who have the final say on policy and towards his operating management committee whose members come to him for decisions on how policy is to be executed. This act of facing both ways should keep him continually aware that, at every level of his co-ordinating hierarchy, the managers have to face both ways. They must attend regular meetings with their superior and also hold regular meetings with their subordinates. Unless this is done, the chain of communication is broken and important areas of detailed decision are neglected. The need for most managers to face both ways does mean, however, that a considerable amount of time must be spent in meetings. Consequently, meetings should be as brief as possible.

There are a number of ways of achieving brevity. One is to be firm and clear about the distinction between co-ordination and detailed execution. A meeting must avoid wasting time on matters which really only concern the detailed administration of one department. Another way is to abide closely by a set of chairmanship rules. The key to participative decision-making lies in the manner in which the managing director chairs his main operating committee and how this style of chairmanship is repeated throughout the business. As a check-list on this process of chairmanship, we give in Figure 6 a set of informal rules. They are described as informal because they are not concerned with the formalities of conducting a meeting, such as reading the minutes, accepting motions, taking votes, recording minutes, etc. Such rules can be found in many small books on sale in most bookshops. What we are concerned with here are the informal rules by which a managing director, or any other chairman of an operating committee, encourages its members to participate in decisions which he, as chairman, must ultimately make on his own responsibility.

Most people respect the co-ordinating authority of someone who knows where he is going and who also enables them to participate in his decision process. His real test will occur, in any case, in the market place. If customers like what the firm does, there cannot be any higher authority—or reward—than this.

Figure 6
INFORMAL RULES OF PARTICIPATIVE DECISION-MAKING

1 Whenever an important subject is to be discussed, the chairman should arrange for the appropriate head of department to prepare a paper for circulation in advance. It need not reach conclusions or even indicate possibilities, but is must summarise the main facts and figures, so that everyone at the meeting can talk to a common background.

2 The chairman should discuss the paper in advance with its author and also separately with another member of the committee, so that he can obtain their instant reactions and test his own ideas on them. He should try to avoid always consulting the same people; he should endeavour to distribute his 'honours' evenly.

3 After the author of the paper has introduced it, the chairman should sum up the problems and the possible solutions, as he sees them, for discussion by the members of the meeting.

4 He should then promote discussion by asking specific questions and he should ensure that, through his questions, everyone present participates. He should take care, in the best 'brainstorming' tradition, not to disccurage comment by dismissing unusual ideas too readily.

5 He may, if appropriate, inject into the discussion 'brinkmanship statements' in which he thinks aloud about the possibility that he will decide to take certain courses of action which might be unpopular, thereby inviting members of the meeting to express the causes of this unpopularity and have them discussed.

6 During the meeting he will, if appropriate, repeatedly sum up the objectives which the committee is trying to achieve.

7 Whenever specific proposals are discussed, the meeting should be invited to suggest examples of where the same or similar ideas can be seen in action.

8 As and when specific points are settled, the chairman should consider whether he ought to sum up what has so far become common ground and what remains to be discussed.

9 Towards the end of the meeting, the chairman should discuss the type of overall decision which is shaping up in his mind and invite further comment.

10 He should then give his decision on the spot, or alternatively state when he expects to make it.

7

Basics of Tidy Administration

Some readers may be starting a new business from scratch, after having spent most of their working lives in a larger organisation where the basics of administration were provided by central service departments. It can be very bewildering suddenly to have to think of everything and take nothing for granted. So we will now pause between the weightier matters of other chapters and present a few guideline notes on basics of administration. These essential services may be so familiar to most readers that their very existence can be overlooked, until they are no longer available from a head office.

First of the basics is the setting up of a company. This can be done by applying directly to the Registrar of Companies. Alternatively, a solicitor or professional accountant or a specialist company registration agent will be pleased to arrange it. Notes on setting up a company will be supplied by the Registrar, Companies House, Crown Way, Maindy, Cardiff, CF4 3UZ, and they will include guidance on seeking approval of a suitable name for the company. This is very important, for the choice of a name can make a considerable difference to the initial image of a business. The name must not be too similar to that of any existing company. It usually pays to look at the lists of registered companies, available to view at Companies House, (at both Cardiff and City Road, London EC1) so that one can study all near-comparisons, rather than just applying blindly for acceptance of a chosen name. Anyone can apply to use his surname in a company name, but this will be approved only if there are one or two other words with it, such as the name of the place of business, in brackets, to distinguish it from other companies using the same surname.

Second among the basics is the raising of capital. Most of the money for a new company should be subscribed as ordinary share capital. There are two major disadvantages in having it in the form of loans. Firstly, the lender may want his loans repaid at a time which is awkward for the company and secondly, it can be a heavy burden on a new company to have to pay interest on loans during the first few years of operation.

Those who supply capital will not be very willing to do so unless they are presented with a clear statement of what the new business aims to do, how much capital it will need, and what sales, cost and profit figures are likely to be achieved month by month during the first year, with broader estimates for perhaps the next couple of years.

A kind of mini prospectus will be needed, but with few words (possibly only a few pages) and many figures. It is more important to demonstrate the prototype product or service than to write masses of words. It is particularly important to present, month by month, very detailed analyses of the expected revenue and the estimated costs. Quite separately, one should also show the cash flow, bearing in mind that there are lags of sometimes a month or more between making a sale and being paid, and also between making a purchase and being expected to pay for it. However, one's credit-worthiness depends on building up a reputation for prompt payment, so late payment of suppliers should not be built into the budget.

The kind of detailed breakdown of a budget required when raising capital for a new business is demonstrated in Chapter 8 and in Appendix III, particularly in Figures 36–9. Revenue forecasts should be broken down by product type, or if there is only one product, by some other criterion such as sales area or channel of distribution. Only when revenue is broken down in such ways can the managing director and those who are being asked to back him have some degree of assurance that the figures presented were not just plucked out of the air. If, for example, the breakdown shows monthly sales for Product A of £xooo in the North West, one can immediately think in terms of who will be able to sell this amount and through which channels of distribution. An experienced capital provider, such as a bank manager, will quickly get down to this kind of reality.

Costs, both direct and overhead, must also be carefully analysed. Unit costs of the goods produced will depend on the volume of production and, if the sales targets are not achieved, this not only means loss of revenue but also, in most cases, higher unit costs. Financial disaster can come quickly if the estimated unit costs prove to be wildly unrealistic.

At the commencement of a business, overhead costs for premises, staff, vehicles and consumables, such as light, heat and stationery, need to be cut as finely as possible. A bank manager will quickly lose interest in a proposition if he thinks it has little chance of supporting its overhead costs. He will see these steadily draining away his bank's cash while the new business is perchance failing to sell up to its full budgeted level.

Third in the basics for setting up a new company's administration is the accounting system. It is extremely important to get this right at the beginning. The chief spoken language of business is words, but the chief written language is figures. By and large, it is true that in a badly run business the staff write each other memos, while in a well run business they send each other figures.

A new business needs to start with a very tidy book-keeping system, however elementary. This means seeking professional advice, but preferably the managing director should not put his personal accountant on the board. Such an action has the disadvantage that his friendly accountant cannot then audit the books. It also leaves open the question whether he is advising the company or directly working for it. Let him remain as a professional accountant, advising the managing director on how to set up the books; however, the MD himself should set them up.

He should initially do the books himself at night if he has the time, so that he knows the detail and can always visualise how it is working out. As soon as possible, he should take on book-keeping help, if only on a part-time basis. There is generally an abundant supply of suitably experienced people, mostly female and married, tidy in their housekeeping at home and ready to devote the same degree of care and attention to keeping accurate books for a business.

One of the traps lying in wait for every new managing director is the idea that bills, etc, can be piled into a drawer until the end of the month and then dealt with all in one evening. A basic rule of accounting is that transactions should be entered up on the day they occur.

It is essential to have a cash book where every payment in or out of the business is entered up each day. If the business is small, in the back of the same cash book it is possible to keep the day book, where non-cash activities such as invoices received and invoices sent are entered up each day.

Tidy cash books and day books provide immediate points of reference if a customer should raise a query; they also make it possible to add the figures up roughly any evening and mark the totals in pencil, to gain an up-to-date picture of the state of the firm's position. Will it have enough cash to pay the impending bills and does it owe more money than it is owed?

Ledgers are also essential if the business deals on a credit basis so that a separate page can be devoted to the firm's transactions with each customer and each supplier. Even in a small business, the sales ledger should generally be a separate book from the bought ledger. Entries in the ledgers need to be made as soon as possible after the day book and cash book entries, so that the books are kept up-to-date and queries from customers or suppliers can be answered with ease.

The last of the five essential account books for the business, which must be kept in good order right from the start, is the nominal ledger. This should preferably be kept initially by the managing director himself, even if he is able to start the business with a book-keeper who looks after all the other books. What the nominal ledger does is to keep the company's account of its own position with regard to the receipt and repayment of capital. If, for example, the shareholders pay in some capital, this is entered in the nominal ledger; when a bank loan is repaid, this is entered. If the MD learns how to keep this book himself, he may only have occasional entries to make, but in making them he will keep himself well acquainted with the capital position.

These five books are basic to a firm's accounting system, and in order to understand fully how they should be used, one needs either to study accountancy or preferably, if time is short, talk in detail to one's accountant. Let him explain the initial books thoroughly instead of just taking them away and producing the accounts himself, thus perpetuating unnecessarily the mysteries of accounting.

The invention of double entry book-keeping was a milestone in history. Its value in preventing simple fraud and ensuring sound sleep for businessmen most nights is so great that it does not deserve to remain a professional mystery.

In addition to keeping the books tidy, it is important to keep the invoices tidy. Invoices received should be serially numbered and entered in the day book and bought ledger and then clipped into an unpaid bills file. When paid, they will be initialled and dated, entered in the cash book and marked 'paid' in the bought ledger, and then clipped into a paid bills file. When making payment a copy of each invoice is preferably sent to the supplier with the cheque so that he does not query the reason for payment. Alternatively, if a statement listing unpaid invoices is received from a supplier at the end of the month this can be returned with the cheque.

When a secretary or clerk types an invoice to send to a customer, it should be serially numbered and she should make at least four copies. The top copy is sent to the customer, one copy is placed in the customer's file, one goes in the typist's day file and the fourth clips into an unpaid invoices file, after its details have been entered in the day book and the sales ledger. If the customer does not pay the bill quickly, he is sent at the end of the month a statement listing all unpaid invoices. When he pays an invoice, this is entered in the cash book and the sales ledger, and the invoice is transferred to a clip for paid invoices.

Wage and salary payments must also be kept very tidily; they must be entered in a book or on pay sheets showing the gross amounts and the various deductions and tax calculations, as instructed in the Inland Revenue booklets. Good stationery shops sell all the necessary books and equipment for systems which ensure that the employee receives a pay slip and the company keeps proper records, both of the individual's pay situation and of the totals of wage and salary payments.

Value added tax must be recorded regularly in separate columns in the right books; the monthly or quarterly VAT return must be completed and a payment of tax made or a refund claimed, as appropriate. The local customs inspector is generally keen to call on any new business and advise on the keeping of books and the making of returns to his requirements.

The need to have all these books for a new business sounds frightening to the beginner, but once he has become used to them, they seem essential and they certainly avoid endless work when trying to backtrack over past events. They also start the business with the right image, so that there need be no trouble with the Inland Revenue, customs officers, suppliers or employees regarding the honesty of the company's dealings. It takes only a few evenings of concentrated effort to learn how to use all these books, but such effort is well worthwhile for the new managing director, if only to save himself from being forever dependent on others who have taken the trouble to learn the essential financial disciplines.

Last but not least in the setting up of a new company's administration is secretarial tidiness. This is almost as important to a new business as its book-keeping. Good filing is particularly vital. Every secretary should make a minimum of three copies of all items typed, the top copy being sent to the addressee, the second copy going into the file of the relevant subject or customer, etc, and the third copy being placed in the day file. The latter, containing everything typed, in date order, provides a second means of reference to earlier correspondence when the subject file containing the second copy is out of the office. It also has another important use. One of the simplest checks that a managing director can make on the progress of his business is to browse through the day file in the evening and see copies of everything which has been typed.

8

Monitoring Performance

THE PROBLEM OF FIGURE-BLINDNESS

Many people of great ability are debarred from the prospect of becoming managing director by the fact that they suffer from figure-blindness. This is an enormous handicap in business. If one cannot follow the figures which show how the company is performing and see them in one's mind's eye whenever there is a quiet moment, it is difficult to use more than a fraction of one's brain capacity in actually solving some of the firm's problems for, generally, these problems can only be summed up in figures.

Are sales adequate? Are costs too high? Are customers paying their bills on time? Is the bank loan too large? These are just a few of the vital questions which can only be asked —and answered—if the relevant figures are fully understood. Failure to understand them is not, however, an incurable fault. The discipline needed to overcome this handicap is relatively easy to acquire.

When a person who is in other respects well educated dismisses figures with a laugh and admits that he only reads the words in a report and takes the figures for granted, this usually means that he is confused by the great variety of layouts of figures presented to him. He has never been able to develop in his mind a picture of figures set out in standard ways that could have instant meaning for him. If the figure-blind are to learn how to read performance figures, they need a set of conventions which will enable them always to see figures in the same relationship to each other.

In the English-speaking world there is a wide variety of layouts for presenting the same types of performance figures, but in Europe, where so many completely different languages are spoken, more care is taken about presenting figures in conventional ways, so that they can be understood even by people who have only a hazy understanding of the words alongside.

There has thus been a gradual build-up, particularly in northern Europe, of a set of conventions for presenting the key figures that enable the performance of a business to be monitored by anyone, regardless of his background, education and training. The steady development of these conventions provides a possible cure for those who suffer from figure-blindness. In this chapter, the nature of these conventions will be discussed and illustrated. They will also be contrasted with the conventions of professional accounting.

A system for monitoring performance is quite different from the professional accounting system. We need to be quite clear about this. The aims of the two systems are different. A universal monitoring system must enable a member of a working team to see regularly figures which enable him to understand:

1 The objectives of the team and his part in achieving them.
2 How much progress is being made towards achieving those objectives.

By contrast, the professional accounting system has several other aims, each of great importance. These include:

1 Protecting the suppliers of capital against fraud.
2 Seeing that the bills are paid by the company to its creditors and to the company by its debtors, and that all other obligations, including wages and taxes, are met.

3 Drawing up an accurate balance-sheet and profit and loss account so that the suppliers of capital know by how much they are better (or worse) off than previously and so that the government knows how much to charge in taxes.

The highly developed double-entry system of checks and balances used in professional accounting and first developed in Italy in the Middle Ages, has clearly quite different aims from a universal monitoring system. The accounting system has proved to be an efficient means of controlling an enterprise whose management may be very autocratic and whose employees may be obedient morons. The accounting system is not essentially geared to provide a means of keeping team members informed of their immediate goals and of how they are performing on the way to these goals.

There is an important workaday distinction to be drawn between the logic of a universal monitoring system for a business and the logic of its accounting system. An essential of accounting is transactional entry. Every transaction of the business must be entered in two separate books. It is entirely sensible that when accounting entries are made by hand, these entries should be placed beneath one another down the page. Various aspects of each entry, such as the date of the entry and perhaps an analysis of it, may be set out in columns side by side, but the entire entry will be confined to one line across the page.

An advantage of making each entry beneath the previous one so that time is moving steadily down the page is that each column can be totalled, in the conventional manner of addition learnt at school. Figure 7a shows typical entries in an accounting system. It does not matter at this point what kind of book is being entered up; all we are concerned with now is that every transaction is entered separately, that the entries are made one below the other so that time moves down the page, and that each aspect of an entry is set out in a separate column.

Serial Number	C O D E	CUSTOMER'S NAME	F O L I O	TOTAL SALES		PRODUCT A		PRODUCT B		
2190	T	H. Bloggs Ltd	7	401	72	241	52	160	20	
2191	M	R. Smith Ltd	59	174	05	174	05			
92	B	S. Johnson Ltd	14	52	41	12	21	40	20	
93	B	R. Jones Ltd	15	41	72	20	32	21	40	
94	T	K. Brown Ltd	8	60	20	41	10	19	10	
95	M	M. Stewart Ltd	60	33	14	14	4	19	10	
96	R	K. Hughes Ltd	12	210	44	161	23	39	21	

Figure 7a Typical entries in an accounting system

Notes on Figure 7a

1 This is actually part of a sales day book, recording every sales transaction in strict order of happening.
2 Each transaction is given a serial number both for reference and to ensure that the proceeds of sales transactions are not subsequently 'lost' and diverted to private purposes.
3 It can be helpful to code each item for quick reference to the source of the sale, for example the publicity mailing which initiated contact with the customer or the salesman who closed the deal.
4 It is usually sufficient to give the name of the customer without his address, for each transaction will also be entered on the ledger page devoted solely to that customer and at the top of that ledger page will be the customer's name and full address, any discounts applicable, and so forth.
5 Total value of the sales transaction is usually entered in the first column and an analysis is made, product by product, in the subsequent columns.
6 Since all the transactions made on the same day are listed together in a day book, the date merely has to be entered above the day's list. By contrast, when these items are also entered in the sales ledger, the date must be entered against each item otherwise there will be no quick way of knowing when the transaction took place. Also, the serial number from the day book will be entered in the ledger so that any disputed item can be quickly identified.

XYZ COMPANY INCOME AND EXPENDITURE, MONTHLY, 1978						
£,000			1	2	3	
SALES REVENUE			4,106	3,982	4,975	
TOTAL EXPEN- DITURE			3,572	3,714	4,185	
PROFIT OR LOSS			534	268	790	

Figure 7b

Notes on Figure 7b

1 The name of the company, what the table records and for what period need to be shown at the top, also the units of money—in this case thousands of pounds.
2 It is unnecessary to write the names of the months at the top of the columns, since everyone knows that January is month 1 in the calendar, February is month 2, and so on. Arabic decimal numbers have the advantage of being almost universally used, whereas words change from language to language.
3 This table records side by side for each month the sales revenue, the total expenditure and the profit or loss. Thus, the trend of these figures can be seen at a glance and there is no need to refer to another sheet for last month's figures.
4 Each month, the person entering up the new month's figures can have his sheet photocopied, with copies being circulated to all who should know these figures. They can then throw away their old copy and substitute it with the new one.

63

By contrast, a universal monitoring system for a business team must be laid out very differently, for it must tell people who work together, in summary form, what they are required to do or have agreed to do. Later it must tell them how well they have done towards meeting their objectives. Therefore, it is concerned with totals and sub-totals, not with individual transactions. Moreover, it should preferably use the same convention for the movement of events through time as is used in the language of story-telling and in charts and graphs. This convention is that time moves from left to right across the page.

Thus, the progress of a business must be shown by figures which are set out in columns across the page, each column representing a period of time such as a month, or a moment of time such as the end of a month. The next column to the right must represent the next period or next date, and so on. Various aspects of the business will be set out down the page, but everything relating to the same period or date will appear in the same column.

Figure 7b shows typical entries in columns, side by side, of the sales revenue, total expenditure and profit of a business in three successive months. This is an elementary example of a universal monitoring system for a business. It aids the reader in visualising figures about the business, as it moves forward through time, and across the page (each column is headed by the number of the month, January being 1, February 2, etc).

The main convention of a universal monitoring system, that time moves from left to right across the page, needs to be treated with as much respect as the main convention of English grammar, that a written statement is laid out as subject, verb, object, in that order. This latter convention is so powerful that the newspaper headline MAN BITES DOG immediately conveys the news that something very unusual has happened. Nobody suspects that a mistake has been made in laying out the words and that really the dog has bitten the man, even though this would be more usual.

The logic of a universal monitoring system for business can claim to be part of the numerical logic of human freedom. This may seem surprising, for throughout history the cause of freedom has been mainly expressed in words and very often by persons who, although not necessarily strong in numerical skills, had great verbal skills capable of arousing the support of large numbers of people. Nevertheless, it is worth looking briefly at why and how human freedom has a numerical logic. This is basic to understanding the need for a universal monitoring system in business.

Why did freedom develop mainly in Europe? Probably because that continent has a temperate climate and, as a result, the land does not need irrigation. Wherever irrigation is needed, there is a case for having an overlord, by whatever name, to control the water supply. Hence there is a temptation for him also to control the people.

Why did individual liberty and its essential system of parliamentary government develop early and strongly in Britain? Probably because in this offshore island the ruler did not even have the excuse that he needed a standing army to keep foreigners at bay. A navy, yes, but of what use is that for controlling the people on shore? A sovereign with no excuse for a standing army was largely dependent on the willing co-operation of the local squires who could quickly form their own militia if they came into fundamental disagreement with him, as they did in seventeeth-century Britain. Hence there was a reasonable chance of evolving a system of basic human rights and elective government. This was first carried to its logical conclusion of one man one vote in the United States, itself an offshoot of the offshore island of the temperate European continent.

It seems clear from history that a numerical logic for human freedom must essentially be the logic of independent self-support. What, in essence, is freedom other than the ability to stand independent of a boss? Why was the farmer in a temperate climate able to stand independent of his ruler? Because he had capital in the form of land, buildings, harvested crops, livestock and implements. He also had an independent water supply. Therefore, he could nourish his family and employees through the whole year, entirely independently, so that they had the capability to fight, if necessary, to maintain their independence.

An important feature of capital is that if one uses it well, it can produce a stream of income over a period of time which provides nourishment. But there is another side to this coin. A stream of income is also the source of accumulated capital, if the whole stream is not consumed as fast as it arrives.

Independence, as an historical development, can thus be seen as substantially a process of acquiring capital in order to produce a stream of income and then regulating the use of that income in order to maintain and hopefully increase the capital. In the past, this could be done by one person or by a medieval manor; nowadays, it can be done by a modern business corporation.

A company cannot expect to preserve its independence unless it builds up and maintains the know-how of the working group. But this know-how lies mainly in the individual team members. Frequent job changes destroy the effectiveness of teamwork, so a corporate team must be a compromise affair. It needs to have special inducements for long service, but these must stand side by side with the basic freedom of the individual to change jobs.

Modern freedom therefore has two separate life-styles. Some individuals can stand on their own feet as small business owners or farmers or talented professionals, such as opera singers and lawyers, but most people need to work in a team. It is important for these people that freedom should have two aspects: the independence of the team as a whole should be preserved, but so also should the freedom of the individual to move from one team to another.

The numerical logic, or numerology of the independent corporate team must express in figures the prospect of the team surviving as an independent organisation through being financially self-supporting. Also, members of the team need to be able to follow out this prospect, in figures, for themselves. The corporate team, as a compromise affair, must recognise the freedom of the individual to change jobs, but it must also encourage members to stay. Among the key inducements to stay will be a sense of participation; this is difficult to achieve unless members know the direction in which the team is going.

Each business sells its products or services and aims to gain enough revenue to cover its expenses with, hopefully, a surplus so that the firm can accumulate more capital and perhaps finance the serving of more customers. The independence of the business depends on covering the expenses and at least some of the time achieving a surplus. A big drop in revenue for any extended period can result either in bankruptcy or in the firm being swallowed up by another business. With its demise goes the right of an independent team to make their own decisions.

The numerology of the independent corporate team must therefore express in figures, for team members to see, the chance of the firm remaining independent. We have, however, seen that independence is related to the possession of capital and that this capital is used in the business to produce a stream of income. If the income is adequate, this is used to increase the store of capital. Therefore, the numerology of the independent corporate team should be in two parts: it must show what is happening to the capital and it must show what is happening to the income.

The capital part must show changes in the capital at the disposal of the corporate team between one date and the next. The income part must show changes in the income and expenditure of the team between one income period and the next. The figures in the two parts of the numerology must obviously have a relationship to each other, which we will now examine.

67

ABC COMPANY BALANCE SHEET, MONTHLY, 1977/78					
£ million		30/4	31/5	30/6	
SOURCE OF FUNDS	Issued ordinary shares	30	30	30	
	Reserves	40	42	52	
	Loan stock	30	30	40	
	TOTAL	100	102	122	
EMPLOYMENT OF FUNDS	Fixed assets	20	19	21	
	Current accounts assets receivable	40	42	54	
	Stocks	30	31	38	
	Work in progress	40	42	48	
	Cash	10	9	14	
	Total current assets	120	124	154	
	Current liabilities Accounts payable	30	31	32	
	Bank loans	10	10	0	
	Total current liabilities	40	41	32	
	Net current assets	80	83	101	
	Net total assets	100	102	122	

Figure 8a

Notes on Figure 8a

1 As this table shows a company's balance-sheet, month by month, the columns must refer to specific dates on which the balance-sheet was drawn up. In this case, it was the last day of the months of April, May and June respectively.

2 The top three rows of the table show the source of funds for the company, in this case the issue of ordinary shares to shareholders, the building up of reserves through reinvesting profits in the business and the issue of loan stock to stockholders. (For simplicity no mention is made of taxation or dividends in this table and the problem of inflation is ignored.)

3 Thus one can see that there was only a slight growth of funds due to the reinvestment of profits of £2 million between April and May but there was a larger build-up between May and June, when £10 million of profits were reinvested and £10 million of additional loan stock issued. In one month there was thus a growth of £20 million in the funds available to the company.

4 How was the money used? The lower rows of the table show that funds were employed in fixed assets such as buildings, machines and vehicles, current assets such as money owed by customers (accounts receivable), stocks of unsold goods and raw materials, and work in progress through the factory and cash, but from these must be subtracted the current liabilities such as money owing to suppliers (accounts payable) and money borrowed from the bank, thus giving the net current assets.

5 The total of funds employed must exactly equal the total of funds made available, if every penny is being accounted for. Hence the totals along the bottom, for 'employment of funds', must equal the totals, month by month, shown for 'source of funds'.

6 This series of balance-sheets starts with the source of funds at the top, because it seems logical to explain the source of funds before explaining how they are being used. However, it is quite common for companies to show first how the funds are being used and then, at the bottom, their source.

Figure 8a shows a series of typical capital statements in the style of the numerology of business. Notice that each column is headed by a specific date, in this case the last day of each successive month. Each of the rows tells us something about either the source of funds available to the corporate team or how those funds are being used by the team on the given date. The source of funds is analysed in a number of rows and then the use of funds is analysed in other rows. Every penny must be accounted for, so in each column the analysis of source of funds must add up to the same total as the analysis of use of funds. However, at the next date shown, the total of capital being used may be different. More capital may have been provided from outside the firm, or the income of the

69

ABC COMPANY INCOME AND EXPENDITURE, MONTHLY, 1977/78					
£ million			4	5	6	
REVENUE	Sales of product product A		30	31	32	
	Sales of product product B		23	24	28	
	Total Revenue		53	55	60	
EXPENDITURE	Over-head expenses		15	16	16	
	Production costs product A	11	11	11	10	
	Production costs product B	14	8	8	10	
	Distribution costs		5	5	6	
	Advertising costs		12	11	8	
	Total operating costs		36	34	34	
	Total expenditure		51	50	50	
.Profit or Loss			2	5	10	

Figure 8b

Notes on Figure 8b

1 As this table shows the company's income and expenditure statement, each column will show the flow of revenue in and of expenditure out of the business during the month indicated. In this case, the months of April, May and June are shown.
2 The rows near the top of the table show the sales revenue from two different products each month and the total sales revenue.
3 Below the revenue are several rows showing various types of expenditure incurred in obtaining the sales revenue.
4 First is shown the overhead expenses such as office staff salary costs, heat and lighting, telephone and mail, stationery, regular maintenance costs and the depreciation of durable assets.
5 Next are shown the costs of producing the amount of product A and product B actually sold each month. The narrow column before the monthly columns begin is used for unit costs. Admittedly, unit costs vary with output. Nevertheless, some acceptable average unit cost must be arrived at in order that, when it is multiplied by the number of units sold, a total direct cost of producing the units actually sold can be obtained and charged as the production cost.
6 Next below are shown the costs of distributing or dispatching the goods sold.
7 Below this are shown the advertising costs actually incurred during these months for the purpose of selling products A and B.
8 Thus it is possible to add up the total operating costs which vary with the quantity sold.
9 To these are added the overhead costs, shown below total revenue, to produce total expenditure
10 When total expenditure is deducted from total revenue, the result is profit or loss.

corporate team during the month may have been greater than its expenditure, so that capital was accumulated. Alternatively, the income may have been less than expenditure so that capital was lost.

We now turn to Figure 8b to learn more of what happened. This shows a series of typical income and expenditure statements in the style of the numerology of business. Notice that each column is now headed by a specific period of time, not a date. In this case, each period is a month and the months are shown in successive columns. Each of the rows now tells us, starting from the top, the sources of income, which may be analysed over several rows and then totalled, and lower down the page, the causes of expenditure, which again may be analysed over several rows and then totalled.

It will be obvious that if Figures 8a and b relate to the same firm's activities over the same period, the numbers must tie up. For example, if Figure 8a shows that between 31 May and 30 June, the capital available to the team increased by £20 million and if it is also clear that only £10 million of this was supplied as new capital from outside the firm, then the other £10 million must have come from customers. During June, revenue from customers must have exceeded expenditure by £10 million. In fact, as Figure 8b shows, it did (in this example we are ignoring taxation and other complicating factors).

Now that we have seen the changes in the capital available to the business team and how these changes relate to the flow of income and expenditure expressed in the conventions of a universal monitoring system, we are in a position to say more about how this relates to human freedom.

Earlier, we were negative about freedom. We implied that there had been an historical struggle for independence and we saw that independence involved having capital in order to obtain an income flow and hence, an independent source of nourishment. It took mankind thousands of years of developing civilisation, aided by geography in the form of temperate zones and islands, to appreciate the relationship between capital and independence.

Once this relationship had been achieved in some prominent, well populated part of the world, the concepts of freedom would be available for others to take up and put into effect in less favourable areas. This, however, is still the negative side of freedom, the obtaining of independence. What is the positive side?

It is surely seen as the ability to dream and plan, to create reality out of a vision. The numerology of human freedom, in so far as it relates to a corporate business, is thus expressed in the ability of the corporate team to plan ahead and spread out their plans in figures which express their aspirations.

Why figures? Most plans also contain words and sometimes drawings, but we are concerned here only with figures. Money is the common language for expressing business activity. A corporate team does not have much freedom unless it can express its aspirations in financial figures for the months ahead and perhaps even for a few years ahead. Numerical statements of aspiration are in practice called budgets. As one would expect from what has already been said, they are divided into capital and income budgets.

Figures 9a and b respectively show capital and income budgets of a business for six months ahead. It will be noticed that the figures are all written on a shaded background. The convention has grown up in Europe that budget figures should be written on a shaded background and the figures of actual operating results should be written on a clear background. This enables everyone to see at a glance which are budget figures and which are actual, without the need for explanatory words. Moreover, the budget and actual figures can be placed next to each other, for easy comparison, without causing confusion. The shaded rows containing the budget figures are always placed immediately above the clear rows showing the actual results for the same period.

Figures 10a and b show the same budget figures as 9a and b, but time has moved on and the actual results for three of the six months shown are now available. It is therefore possible to compare actual figures with budget figures for these months, on a month by month basis.

When comparing actual figures with budget, month by month, one is interested to know whether the ups and downs of business life are evening out so that the general result over a period of months will be much the same as budgeted, or is the position getting steadily worse, or steadily better? What is the trend?

This can be seen by filling in the cumulative figures, from one month to another. There cannot, of course, be a 'cumulative' capital statement, since a capital statement already adds up the capital. Cumulative figures can be provided only for an income and expenditure statement, where the income from one month to another can be totalled and likewise so may the

PQR COMPANY CAPITAL BUDGETS 1978						
£,000	1	2	3	4	5	6
Buildings	5	4	3	20	4	2
Vehicles	1	2	1	3	4	1
Furniture and fittings	1	1	1	0	0	0
Project A	7	6	7	0	0	0
Project B	0	0	3	4	20	5
TOTAL	14	13	15	27	28	8

Figure 9a

Notes on Figure 9a

1 Budget figures are always set out on a shaded background, to distinguish them from actual figures, which are set on a plain one.
2 Capital budget figures represent the amounts of money which it has been agreed can be spent on the items shown. Even though the money has been agreed, it is normal procedure in business that specific projects should be approved as and when they are ready for approval; there are many factors to consider in capital expenditure besides the amount of money (eg, the type of vehicles, where vehicles are being bought).
3 Actual capital expenditure may vary from budget either because its timing is different or because the amounts are different. For example, a new vehicle which has been ordered may not be ready for delivery in the month that it has been entered in the capital budget; also, the model finally approved may differ from the model for which a provisional figure was entered in the budget. Nevertheless, if capital budgets are prepared with care, they can give a useful guide to the amount of money likely to be needed for capital expenditure.
4 This table gives examples only and is not meant to be all-inclusive. It does not, for example, include any figures for machinery. Also it does

PQR COMPANY INCOME AND EXPENDITURE BUDGETS 1978		1	2	3	4	5	6
PROJECT A	Revenue	50	55	47	59	61	63
	Expenditure	40	43	48	48	51	50
	Profit or loss	10	12	-1	11	10	13
PROJECT B	Revenue	70	65	57	71	70	72
	Expenditure	61	57	51	59	60	58
	Profit or loss	9	8	6	12	19	14
TOTAL	PROFIT OR LOSS	19	20	5	23	20	27

Figure 9b

not include any figures for increased working capital other than what is needed for the launching of projects A and B.

5 To the layman, it may seem difficult to estimate the amount of working capital needed for a new project. However, this is no major problem to an accountant. He looks at each item of revenue and each item of operating expenditure which has been budgeted, month by month. He adjusts each to allow for the time taken for bills to be paid—both to the company and by the company. Some items of expenditure, such as wages, have to be paid the same month as they are incurred. Others, such as expenditure on supplies, may not have to be paid until the following

month or even later. Also, some customers pay their bills promptly while others do not. The accountant converts revenue and expenditure budgets into cash flow budgets. The accumulated net outflow of cash, month by month, is the increase in working capital which must be budgeted for. Cash flow is discussed in more detail in Appendix III.

6 If a capital budget statement is absolutely comprehensive, the figures from it should be capable of being taken and added to the actual balance-sheet for the current date, to produce a pro forma balance-sheet for a future date. This is also discussed in Appendix III.

Notes on Figure 9b

1 The budget figures are set on a shaded background, with clear space underneath for insertion of the actual results.

2 The budgets for two separate projects are shown, the totals of both budgeted revenue and budgeted expenditure being given.

3 These totals will have been made up from typical 'building bricks'. For example, if project A is expected to bring in £50,000 revenue in January, this could be because the net price of the product, after average discounts, is £5 and it is estimated that 10,000 units will be sold.

4 How is it estimated that 10,000 units will be sold? Perhaps only because the company knows the number sold last month and last January and has ideas on whether the market now is likely to be better or worse; or again, the salesmen or branches handling this product may have been asked how much more or less they expect to sell than in a known previous period. A combination of all their estimates may be a useful guide to the sales director in making a final estimate.

5 What if the product is new and there is no previous record to go by? The estimate will then be less reliable. If there is a competitive product to compare with, any market research evidence or general trade news on how well it is selling helps to make the company's own estimate more reliable.

6 In estimating expenditure there are two separate problems. The first of these is overheads: the cost of space, staff and other overheads can be estimated from previous experience of these costs, once the size of space, number of staff, etc, are agreed. One of the biggest problems here is to think of everything. Accountants know from their professional training and experience virtually all the types of cost likely to be incurred, though there could be some item special to a particular type of business, which will not be obvious to a young accountant.

7 The second problem is direct operating costs. These vary with the amount sold and the amount produced. Both the unit cost of selling and the unit cost of producing can vary. Nevertheless, some effort must be made to establish average unit costs, so that the quantities sold can be multiplied by the average unit costs in order to produce an estimate of the cost of goods sold. The only direct operating expenditures entered in the income and expenditure statement are those incurred on the goods or services actually sold. All other operating costs must be carried forward, in the value of either stocks or work in progress, and shown in the balance sheet as assets. They cannot be charged as expenditure until the relevant products are either sold or written off as unsaleable.

8 If all expenses were charged as and when they occurred, income and expenditure statements could be rather meaningless. The 'profit' would vary sharply, according to how the invoices arrived. A particular month in which six months' supply of raw materials arrived could show a great loss while the next five months could look misleadingly profitable.

£,000	1	2	3	4	5	6
Buildings	5	4	3	20	4	2
	4	5	3			
Vehicles	1	2	1	3	4	1
	1	2	1			
Furniture and fittings	1	1	1	0	0	0
	1	0	2			
Project A	7	6	7	0	0	0
	7	5	6			
Project B	0	0	3	4	20	5
	0	0	2			
TOTAL	14	13	15	27	28	8
	13	12	14			

Figure 10a

Notes on Figure 10a

1 This table repeats the capital budget shown in Figure 9a but it shows three months of actual performance figures, entered below the budget figures for the same months.
2 Thus it is possible to make immediate comparison, month by month, between actual performance and budget figures, as and when the performance figures become available.

PQR COMPANY INCOME AND EXPENDITURE BUDGET AND ACTUAL FIGURES 1978							
	£,000	1	2	3	4	5	6
PROJECT A	Revenue	50	55	47	59	61	63
		51	58	53			
	Expenditure	40	43	48	48	51	50
		41	48	58			
	Profit or loss	10	12	−1	11	10	13
		10	10	−5			
PROJECT B	Revenue	70	65	57	71	70	72
		71	67	61			
	Expenditure	61	57	51	59	60	58
		62	60	58			
	Profit or loss	9	8	6	12	10	14
		9	7	3			
TOTAL	Profit or loss	19	20	5	23	20	37
		19	17	−2			

Figure 10b

Notes on Figure 10b

1 This table repeats the income and expenditure budget shown in Figure 9b but it shows three months of actual performance figures, entered below the budget figures for the same months.
2 Thus it is possible to make immediate comparison, month by month, between actual performance and budget figures, as and when the performance figures become available.

78

PQR COMPANY INCOME AND EEXPENDITURE BUDGET AND ACTUAL FIGURES, 1978

	£,000	1	2	3	4	5	6
PROJECT A	Revenue	50	55	47	59	61	63
		51	58	53			
			105	152	211	272	335
			109	162			
	Expenditure	40	43	48	48	51	50
		41	48	58			
			83	131	179	230	280
			89	147			
	Profit or loss	10	12	-1	11	10	13
		10	10	-5			
			22	21	32	42	55
			20	15			
PROJECT B	Revenue	70	65	57	71	70	72
		71	67	61			
			135	192	263	333	405
			138	198			
	Expenditure	61	57	51	59	60	58
		52	60	58			
			118	169	228	288	346
			122	180			
	Profit or loss	9	8	6	12	10	14
		9	7	3			
			17	23	35	45	59
			16	19			
TOTAL	Profit or loss	19	20		23	20	37
		19	17	-2			
			39	44	67	87	124
			36	34			

Figure 11

Notes on Figure 11

1 Because the month by month figures do not always make it immediately obvious as to the trend of actual performance, when compared with budget, Figure 11 repeats Figure 10b but also shows how the cumulative figures, month by month, can be filled in.
2 The cumulative figures for both actual performance and budget help to make it immediately obvious whether actual performance is merely varying up and down around the budgeted level or whether it is moving progressively further away from it.
3 To avoid the confusion of having too many figures on a page, it is common practice to accumulate only totals and key items.

expenditure from month to month be totalled. Figure 11 shows the same income and expenditure statement as Figure 10b, but with cumulative totals filled in. Thus it can be seen that the corporate team is doing steadily better than budget, as regards income, and also steadily worse than budget, as regards expenditure. There is more income but also more expenditure. Alas, the increase in income is not as great as the increase in expenditure, so the actual surplus of income accumulated during the first three months is not as great as budgeted for.

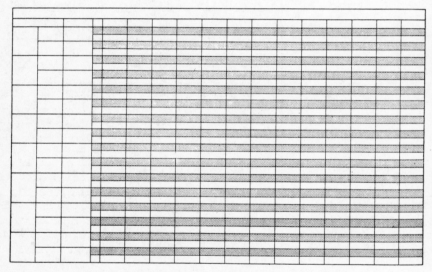

Figure 12 Standard layout planning and control sheet

Notes on Figure 12

1 This table shows the full width of a planning and control sheet, with thirteen monthly columns, to allow either for the firm which uses calendar months or for the firm which uses thirteen accounting periods of four weeks in a year.
2 This same sheet can be used for weekly figures where necessary, as in retail sales. As there are thirteen weeks in a quarter, one sheet will hold a quarter's figures.
3 This same sheet can also be used to show yearly figures for a run of years.

It is an accepted convention that cumulative figures are shown below the month by month figures. To prevent the creation of a mass of confusing numbers, cumulative figures are sometimes left out of the detailed analyses of income and expenditure, but they are filled in for the totals of income and expenditure and for the profit or loss.

To simplify this description of the numerology of business, we have so far shown only part of each specimen document. However, Figure 12 illustrates a full thirteen-column planning and control sheet used in a universal monitoring system for corporate enterprise. It is A4 size, for ease of photocopying, circulation and filing purposes. This sheet was first developed in the early 1960s by Verlag Moderne Industrie in Munich. The style of it can, of course, be simulated on a computer print-out.

Why thirteen columns, not twelve? Because some companies find it more convenient to have thirteen periods of four weeks in a year rather than twelve calendar months. Most companies use calendar months, but a thirteen-column sheet suits either method. Moreover, in some industries such as retailing, it is important to have a weekly comparison of actual results against budget. As there are thirteen weeks in a quarter, a thirteen-column sheet can present a whole quarter of weekly figures.

We mentioned earlier that the multitude of languages in Europe has aided the development of a universal monitoring system. Whereas English-speaking peoples have been able to take a casual attitude to the presentation of figures, knowing that almost everyone could read the words which explained them, the continentals have found it advantageous to develop certain conventions which everyone would understand, without having to know more than a bare minimum of words. The influence of language on these developing conventions can be seen by summarising them as follows:

1 Time always moves from left to right across the page, as in graphs and as in printed sentences which use one of the Western alphabets. By contrast, when figures are presented to people in the English-speaking world, time sometimes runs down the page and sometimes from right to left. All very confusing to the person who is not a 'natural' with figures!

2 Budget figures are always presented on a shaded background, to distinguish them from actual results, which are always presented on a clear background. Budget figures are also presented immediately above the relevant actual figures. Thus it is possible to see at a glance how one is actually performing by comparison with the agreed budget for the same period. By contrast in the English-speaking world, budget figures are sometimes presented alongside the actual figures and sometimes on a separate sheet.

3 Cumulative figures for the year to date are presented immediately below the month by month or week by week figures and space is usually left for them, even when they are not filled in. Looking across a page from left to right, one can see from the monthly and cumulative figures the immediate history of the operation. Is it on budget, or ahead, or behind? If it is performing below budget, is the situation getting cumulatively worse, or is it likely to come right? By contrast, in the English-speaking world, cumulative figures are often presented on a separate page or, if on the same page, they inhibit the presentation of more than one month's figures, so one has to look back over other pages to see the trend.

We may now end this chapter by summarising the general principles of a universal monitoring system:

1 Budgeting is a means of time-sequencing of a corporate team's plans for the future, their likely cost and the income that is expected to be generated. The universal monitoring

system provides a logical layout of a budget as a form of common language between people concerned with the same organisation.

2 The budgeting process is a means of agreeing on what has to be done and then supervising it so that, as far as possible, it is done. A good budgeting system is both a means of decision-making and a means of communication within a working organisation.

3 A budget is a means of granting human freedom while at the same time restraining it in order to achieve the agreed purposes of the team. Each department which is given a budget thereby achieves a certain amount of freedom of decision and action within the given limits, but the budget also expresses in figures the part which this department is expected to play in the overall team effort.

4 Useful budgets are rarely constructed out of thin air. They arise from past experience (eg, what happened last year or recently), with variations applied to express any expected changes from the past. They are made up of 'building bricks' such as unit costs and prices, quantities expected to be produced and quantities likely to be sold.

5 The regular comparison of actual performance against budget is the basic tool for continually reviewing the work of a corporate team, how successful it is in making an independent contribution to human society and what changes, if any, should be considered for its future activity.

6 The universal monitoring system, with its budgeting process, provides a means of enabling each part of the corporate team to know its own role in the total task and how this role fits into the total task, without having to know the details of other roles. A total corporate budget can be broken down into sections and each unit within the total team can be given its own detailed, agreed budget, plus one or more link-budgets showing how this fits into the total picture.

7 The process of preparing and agreeing budgets and of

subsequently watching performance against budget is the ultimate in meaningful participation by members of a corporate team in the decision-making of the firm. Only when plans and actual performance are expressed in financial figures is there a common currency for meaningful participation.

8 The universal monitoring system is capable of being taught at school, alongside the grammar of language. In the workaday world, these two sets of conventions are possibly of equal importance, one for figures and the other for words. In fact, to teach people a set of conventions for words without teaching them a similar set of conventions for figures is to put them at the mercy of those who are naturally good at figures and to make meaningful participation in teamwork very difficult.

Really effective teamwork is hardly possible unless the members of a corporate team have a common understanding of budget layouts and the comparison of actual performance against budget. Without such understanding, some members of the team are 'flying blind' and therefore apprehensive of what is ahead of them. In these circumstances there cannot be an adequate basis of trust between team members.

9 Unless there is a universal monitoring system, all forms of joint consultation are apt to descend into an argument about side issues which everybody does understand, such as the state of the washrooms. A universal monitoring system provides a discipline for reminding everyone of the key questions: where are we trying to go and how successful have we been so far at trying to get there?

10 The monitoring system of a corporate team is completely dependent on the formal accounting system for its supply of accurate figures. Provision of a monitoring system does not usually involve any significant extra cost, but rather it involves the presentation of information which is already available, in a form appropriate to team motivation.

Readers who want to pursue the application of a universal monitoring system of a business organisation should turn to Appendix III. This is based on a real business and it presents figure layouts for eighteen key aspects of a firm's performance. Notes are attached to each presentation.

9

Recognising Personal Achievement

A managing director can make or mar the whole future of his business for years to come by his degree of success in selecting people for key jobs. This is equally true whether he is appointing someone from inside or from outside the firm. The process of selection is widely considered to be a flair which goes with a certain type of personality. Perhaps it is to some extent, but we cannot teach flair in a book. The best we can do is to set out the disciplines involved in selecting people. They are described here in the circumstances of making an appointment from outside the firm because this is usually the situation when one starts by knowing less about the potential candidates for the vacant post. Nevertheless, the same disciplines are for the most part applicable to inside appointments.

These disciplines can never guarantee 100 per cent success in selecting a suitable person for each job, but they can reduce the number of mistakes. They can also increase the chance of making some really outstanding appointments.

The first step in good selection of staff is accurate job description. One cannot accurately describe a job for a potential applicant until one can answer these questions:

1 What will be his job title?
2 To whom will he report?

3 For what organisations, territories, equipment or people will he be responsible?
4 What is the main purpose of the job, in terms of objectives to be achieved?
5 What are the supplementary objectives?
6 What financial and other limits on authority apply to the job?
7 What attendances at meetings are required?
8 Who will be his immediate subordinates?

The second step in good selection is accurate job evaluation. This should define a salary range and other benefits for the job-holder, after one has answered these questions:

1 What particular forms of expertise, in the way of knowledge, know-how or skill are needed in the job?
2 What levels of expertise and experience are needed in relation to his superior? For example, must he be almost ready to take over from the boss or should he merely have qualifications in the same profession, such as a newly qualified accountant joining the staff of an experienced finance director?
3 How capable and experienced must the job-holder be at the following four basic management skills: planning, persuading, monitoring and motivation?

It will not have gone unnoticed that three of the earlier chapters of this book were entitled: Motivation by Money, Planner or Persuader? and Monitoring Performance. These chapters discussed the basic management skills of planning, persuading, monitoring and motivation. At first sight, it might seem that motivation is not a skill, but rather an attribute of personality. However, the researches and training activities of the Harvard Professor of Psychology, David C. McClelland, have made it reasonable to assume that motivation is, to some extent, a skill which can be taught. Chapters 13–16 set the background of financial reward against which it is claimed that personal motivation can most effectively operate, but the right setting is not enough if people do not have the ability and the will to undertake tasks without being continually goaded.

Training in the four basic management skills can be, to some extent, mutually reinforcing. For example, one's motivation is likely to be reinforced through becoming any of the following:

1 Better at planning, so that there is a clear goal ahead.
2 Better at persuading, so that others are co-operative towards achieving the goal.
3 Better at monitoring, so that one knows how much of the distance towards the goal has already been achieved.

To take another example, one's desire to learn the techniques of monitoring performance is likely to be increased if one is highly motivated and has established clear-cut plans and persuaded people to co-operate in executing them. In these circumstances, the next logical question is likely to be: how well are we performing against target? Or again, a highly motivated 'backroom boy', good at planning and creative work and skilled at monitoring performance, is likely to be aware of whether he needs to become a more effective persuader. Or yet again, a well motivated 'personality man' who is very good at handling people, an effortless persuader and a ceaseless monitor, is likely to be aware of whether he needs more skill at planning the future of the business.

The author attaches considerable weight to the inclusion of these four basic management skills in a job evaluation system and also in a performance appraisal system. Anyone can make up a list of qualities required in a job-holder, if one thinks of words such as initiative, enthusiasm, loyalty, co-operation and reliability, The trouble with such lists, if included in a system, is that they result in extremely subjective judgements. The four basic management skills tend to be more objective because they add up to a logical summation of what managers do and also because it is, to some extent, possible to train people in them.

The third step in good selection is effective recruitment. This is most important because it is easy to select a bad candidate from a bad bunch of candidates, but it is not so easy to go wrong if all the candidates are of high quality. To obtain good recruits, one might have to advertise in the right national, local, trade or professional media, or to engage the services of a specialised recruitment agency. It is to be hoped that all such efforts are merely a back up in case one cannot recruit a known candidate and that one has already been watching talent in the same industry or profession. Better the devil you know than the devil you don't know. When no good candidates arise from personal contacts, advertising or from the use of specialised recruitment agencies, it is sometimes better to postpone making an appointment than to accept an unsatisfactory candidate.

The fourth stage in good selection is choosing the short-list of candidates for interview. This is not made much easier or more reliable if candidates have to fill in a pre-printed application form; indeed, application forms are not generally a good idea. It is better to let candidates apply in their own style, including in their application any specific facts asked for in the job advertisement.

If a candidate is sent an application form in advance, he is put in control of the situation because he can take his time in shaping up answers in favourable ways. A detailed application form may prove to be more a test of the candidate's ability at filling in application forms than of his ability at doing the job under offer.

By contrast, an interview form puts the employer in control, for he completes the form during the course of the interview and each question takes the candidate by surprise. It is therefore possible to structure the interview in such a way as to break through the particular image of himself which each candidate likes to build, and so get closer to the actual facts.

In selecting short-list candidates for interview, it is advisable to draw up a comparative list of all applicants except those with obvious shortcomings in relation to the requirements of the job. This comparative list should make it possible to see where vital pieces of information are missing and to pursue them. It should also make it possible to rule out some candidates whose shortcomings relative to others would not necessarily be obvious when looked at singly.

A typical comparative list will have the names of candidates down the left-hand side, entered in order of arrival of application, with the columns across the top, headed by such subjects as: present employer; number of years with him; present location; present job title; present salary plus bonus; age, sex, marital status; qualifications and education; previous employer; number of years with him; experience and abilities of special relevance to the job applied for.

Making out a comparative list takes very little time and it is one of the best ways of concentrating attention on what the applicants actually said. Most of the facts can be entered very quickly, once they have been given, but the last item on the above list may require more intensive searching amongst the information supplied. Time spent on this is usually well spent, for it is right at the heart of the matter. What special experience and abilities do the applicants have which are relevant to the job? Once these have been summarised and compared, short-listing is likely to be quicker and more accurate.

The fifth stage in good selection is interviewing the short-listed candidates. What are the real facts which must be obtained in an interview? These can be sought by using the kind of 'model' interview form given in Figure 13 at the end of this chapter. It should be treated only as a model and adapted to suit the needs of recruitment in particular industries and in particular functions such as marketing, production, finance, personnel, research and development.

Before beginning the serious interview, an employer should

greet the candidate with pleasantries aimed at putting him at ease. Unless this is done, there is only a limited chance of obtaining really candid answers to questions. The most suitable pleasantries are those which show real interest in the candidate because they are based on information which he has already supplied in his job application.

If necessary, the pleasantries may be extended by discussing personal facts which are needed, but which may not have been already supplied, such as the ages and sexes of his children. By the time these are completed, the candidate should be as much at ease as he is ever likely to be.

The remainder of the interview should then cover three broad subjects: firstly, what experience the candidate has had and how successful he has been in this work; secondly, what the employer requires of the successful candidate and where the vacant post fits into the purpose and activities of the firm; thirdly, how the candidate's experience and abilities are likely to match up to the firm's requirements.

The first stage is covered in detail by the interview form in Figure 13. It will be seen that this form is designed to analyse the applicant's work experience in each recent job, in terms of:

1 The job responsibilities and objectives.
2 The specialised know-how required.
3 The basic management skills required.
4 The performance actually achieved in relation to target or objective.

The second stage of the interview, describing the firm's requirements, will be an enlargement of the job description and job evaluation. This is deliberately a second stage, not a first. The candidate should tell his own story first, without too much aid in shaping it towards the firm's requirements.

The third stage can only be initiated at a first interview. If a candidate seems to be a good prospect for the job, both employer and candidate will want to think seriously and then meet again to discuss whether the candidate's experience and abilities match up to the firm's requirements. Has he the right level and type of knowledge and experience for the job; has he the necessary skills at planning, persuading, monitoring and motivation?

Immediately after the first interview, the summary at the top of the interview form is completed. By then, the employer should already have a fair idea of whether he wants to see the candidate again.

A second interview is absolutely essential before making an appointment. Impressions and attitudes are likely to be different the second time. Would the employer and the candidate really get on well? If they are hoping to work together for years, two looks at each other in advance are not extravagant.

The sixth stage in choosing the right candidate is the taking up of references. When candidates are at management level this is best done by telephone. The first questions put to a referee should merely check the basic facts. Did the candidate work for the referee at a specified salary level between specified dates and with certain specific responsibilities? After this fact-checking, the employer can ask: 'Would you employ Mr X again?' It is difficult for anyone to avoid giving a positive or negative answer to this question, but if it is avoided, the evasive answer can be followed up by a supplementary question.

When a really good candidate is interviewed twice, it is tempting to forego the taking up of references. What could they possibly reveal? By this time the employer may be unwilling to have anything said against a good candidate, though some surprising things are revealed through the taking up of references. Better to be sure than sorry. The objective is to appoint someone who is good at the job, not someone who may be merely good at interviews. The real facts can only be attained by exercising all the disciplines of the selection process.

Sometimes the job is offered to the chosen candidate before references have been taken up. In these circumstances, it is important to make the offer conditional on the references being satisfactory. When it is almost 100 per cent certain that a candidate has nothing to hide, there is advantage in taking up references late, after the candidate has given in his notice to his present employer. Then it may be possible to approach the present employer for a reference. This is likely to be warm-hearted towards a person whom the previous employer is sorry to lose, but it may possibly include one or two useful points of realism.

The letter confirming a verbal offer of a job to the success-ful candidate should conform to the requirements of a legal employment contract and be complete, including all conditions of employment. It is a very great let-down to an employer's image if he sends an outline job offer and subsequently, after the candidate has committed himself to coming, sends a full offer including onerous conditions of employment of which the candidate had had no previous warning.

Finally, details of the appointed candidate should be entered in the firm's personnel records, and the appropriate informa-tion supplied to the accounts department for pay purposes. It is important to the reputation of a firm as a good employer that it should maintain full and accurate personnel records so that it can keep faith with its commitments to employees. Where a firm is not big enough to have a personnel depart-ment, the managing director must have a confidential secre-tary or assistant who can at least keep a separate personnel cabinet, with a file on each employee.

One copy of every job offer letter should go in the file of the person appointed. As the other copy cannot go in the normal day file of all letters typed because of its confidential nature, it should best go in a special day file which is readily available to the managing director. This way he can, at a glance, keep abreast of all current job offers and all current employment contracts. He also needs to be able to use previous offers as a basis for writing new ones. He should never dictate a job offer without preparation for fear of leaving out some vital clause. There is hardly a quicker way to lose credence with a potential employee than to overlook an important detail of his employment contract.

Good personnel records are the key to ensuring that commitments to employees are not overlooked. Figure 41 in Appendix III shows the standard planning and control sheet, which was discussed in Chapter 8, adapted as an employee pay and benefits record. Details of the employee, such as name and address, date of birth, date of joining the firm and national insurance number, are entered at the top of the form, which is then clipped to the inside front cover of the employee's personnel file. The columns across the body of the form represent years, moving from left to right. The side headings are concerned with such matters as basic salary or wage, salary points if a points scale is used, bonus, total earnings, pension, car if relevant, membership of a health insurance scheme, life cover, and other forms of reward or benefit, including allocations under an employee share scheme.

In some companies, it may be preferred to print the employee pay and benefits record on the back of a personnel card which contains much other information. The layout of the card is important and the author strongly recommends the layout of Figure 41 so that this record conforms to the convention that time moves from left to right across the page. As we shall discuss in Chapter 13, earnings progression is an important part of employee motivation. When reviewing an employee's financial progress, it is helpful to all concerned if the figures are laid out in the same style as if one is reviewing the progress of a company or a department. The style of Figure 41 can, of course, be programmed into a computer print-out.

The form should provide a permanent, instantly readable record of the employee's financial progress during his career with the firm. If actual payments and benefits are entered in the clear areas, forward commitments such as entry to a pension scheme or eligibility for a pay increase can be entered in the shaded areas. Such commitments should also, however, be entered in a personnel diary so that the person responsible for the firm's personnel records can make a daily check that all reviews and promises are fulfilled. When they are, they can then be struck through in the diary and initialled as implemented, the decisions taken being recorded on the employee's pay and benefits record. All other relevant action, such as informing the accounts department and sending a confirming letter to the employee, if necessary, will be effected at the same time.

Personnel matters take time, but they are worthwhile in order to have a contented team of employees who can concentrate on their real jobs. The time spent can be kept within reasonable bounds if there is a tidy personnel record system maintained by a person who is proud of his 'good housekeeping'.

Wherever possible, job vacancies should be filled by promotion from within the company. It is difficult to do this on a fair basis unless there is a system of individual performance appraisal. Morale is quickly destroyed if employee talent is overlooked when promotion opportunities arise. An appraisal system is also an essential basis for the training and development of potential abilities. It will usually be conducted annually but in some industries, by the nature of the work, it is better done twice a year.

Appraisal will normally be carried out by an employee's immediate boss who will discuss the results with his superior before also discussing them with the employee himself. At junior levels, the type of appraisal system needed will depend on the nature of the industry and, in some cases, a suitable system is available through the relevant trade association. At senior levels of management, however, the method of performance appraisal needed will be much the same, regardless of the type of industry.

It is the author's experience that, at these levels, performance appraisal should generally be divided into three parts. About 60 per cent of the total score should be awarded for performance against budget, target or objectives previously set; about 20 per cent should be awarded for progress in keeping up-to-date in a specialist trade or profession; the remaining 20 per cent or thereabouts should be divided equally between awards for demonstrated management skill in the four basic areas of planning, persuading, monitoring and motivation.

This kind of distribution of points makes it clear to the managers appraised that their primary task is to achieve their budget, target or objectives, but if they experience a poor year for reasons not entirely explainable, at least they can hope to score some fairly good marks for keeping up-to-date and for being a good, all-round manager, in terms of the four basic skills.

At the time of discussing the appraisal with the employee, the need for any training or experience which will enable him to improve his performance should be discussed with him and noted on the appraisal form, without making any extravagant commitments. This is also a good time to discuss and note the employee's long-term career aspirations and his immediate aims regarding both job responsibilities and rewards.

It is not enough for an employer to identify personal achievement; he must show that it is recognised both in the rewards paid and in praise for specific accomplishments. Praise for successes and criticism of failures should always be specific. General praise is mere flattery and general criticism is destructive of motivation. Specific praise is always a boost to motivation and specific criticism can usually be made in a manner which gives a boost to both the desire to learn and the will to work.

Figure 13
INTERVIEW FORM

(Note: This form should not be given to the applicant for completion. Its value lies in assessing the applicant's instant reaction to the questions. Use this form as a basis for analysing the applicant even if you have invited him to apply and have known him for years. Start wth his name and address and complete the summary immediately after the interview is over.)

Summary

Assessment on five point scale   Interviewer
(*1 = highest*)

Date   Position as

Division, subsidiary, branch or area of employment
Comments

Brief description of your overall impression

Assessment of previous experience

Assessment of previous career

Assessment of potential for development

What are his strengths and weaknesses?

What, if anything, should be investigated further?

Name   Telephone No

Address

Opening Questions
(Observation: Did the candidate come to the interview prepared and with definite ideas? He may well behave similarly if he joins the company.)

What especially appealed to you about our advertisement (or job description)?

What do you already know about our company?

Are you at present in employment where you   Yes☐   No☐
have not given or been given notice?

When was notice given?

Why are you dissatisfied with your present employment?

What are you looking for in your next position?

What do you hope to achieve during the next few years?

Business Experience
(Important: Go through all his previous jobs and get as accurate a picture as possible of his activities and positions held. If the applicant is evasive or glosses over some important point, try to get at the facts. It is best to start with his present job and work backwards.)

Present or latest position (Job No 1)

Company

Industry and products

Since when employed by them?

Job title	Present salary/total income
Since when?	Position on entry to firm and salary/total income
Reason for promotion?	Reason for lack of promotion?

Responsibilities
(for organisations, territories, products, equipment, people)

Objectives (main and subsidiary)

Achievements
(in relation to objectives, targets, budgets, specific projects)

Know-how required
(special knowledge, skill, experience)

Management skills
(specific work experience in planning, persuading, monitoring or motivation)

Opinions of company and your superior

What would you do differently?

(Important: Compare the answers to the above questions with the reason given for wishing to make a change of job. Do they substantiate any criticisms made or are they contradictory?)

Previous position (Job No 2)
(Ask the same questions as before)

Reason for changing employer/job

Starting salary/total income   Final salary/total income

Previous position to that one (Job No 3)
(Ask the same questions as before)

Reason for changing employer/job

Starting salary/total income   Final salary/total income

Other jobs held

Company	Your job title and responsibilities	Starting salary	Final salary	Reason for changing
4				
5				
6				

Personal motivation

What was the real reason for your becoming a ....?
(Job No 1)

Have all your expectations been   Which have not been fulfilled?
fulfilled?

What do you consider to be your strong points as a ....?
(Job No 1)

Which aspects don't appeal to you so much?

Background/Education/Private Life

Date of birth	Place of birth	Country	Father's occupation

School or college, etc	Town	From	To	Exams passed on leaving
1				
2				
3				
4				

Reasons for leaving full-time education early or not pursuing studies,
if relevant

Military service	From	To	☐None	Final rank

Married	☐Yes	☐No	Occupation of wife (now or previous)

101

Age and sex of children *(eg 3F = girl aged 3)*	House owner? ☐Yes ☐No

Total mortgage and other debt commitments, if relevant

Car owner? ☐Yes ☐No	Type of vehicle

Mobility and flexibility	Class of driving licence

How much time do you now spend yearly abroad on business? What is the maximum you would find acceptable?

How many nights do you now spend weekly/monthly away from home?	What is the maximum you would find acceptable?

How many hours overtime weekly do you now work?	Would you work occasionally at weekends?

Would you be prepared to move home?	At short notice/only after some time?

Detailed current earnings

£	+ £
Annual basic salary	Average commission/or bonus pa

+£	=
Annual value of other fringe benefits	Total annual income

Current expenses (eg daily allowance, hotel allowance, mileage rate)

Company car ☐No ☐Yes	Make, type and engine capacity

102

Arrangement re private use

Income required £ _____

How much must you earn from the start?

Why must you earn more than at present?	Approx earnings expected after a year

What questions do you wish to ask us?
(Important: Pay special attention to systematic, logical questioning by the applicant. Can he distinguish between important and unimportant matters? Is he sufficiently interested in the company, its products, its marketing methods, its technology, its financial position, its development potential? Is he quick on the uptake and does he show critical judgement? How quickly did he concentrate on the personal financial aspects? When you have finished speaking, encourage him to summarise for you what you have told him. Did he grasp the essentials?)
Observations

Final Questions

Normal notice period required	Could you possibly be available earlier?

Decision: How soon must you hear from us? Also when can you let us have a decision?

Alternatives: Are you negotiating elsewhere at present? How attractive are the offers?

Further interview: ☐Unnecessary	☐Desired

Suitable date/time	Advise by (date)

References: (two names, addresses and telephone numbers, with job titles, one of whom should be a current or previous employer.)

(Reassure the applicant where relevant, that no contacts will be made without first checking with him that it is all right.)

10

Coping with the Trade Cycle

WHEN TO POSTPONE NEW PROJECTS

It was the great American author, Ralph Waldo Emerson, who said:

> If a man write a better book, preach a better sermon or make a better mouse-trap than his neighbour, though he build his house in the woods, the world will make a beaten path to his door.

Anyone wishing to give Emerson a 'yes, but' answer could fairly say: 'Yes, but not during the downward phase of the trade cycle'.

One of the businessman's selling problems is to try to come into the market with his better mouse-trap when there is a shortage of ordinary traps. In order to survive, he must see that he is not caught with heavily extended credit in the midst of launching a new mouse-trap when the market for ordinary traps is over-supplied and they are being sold off at cut prices.

The prospects of survival for the independent business enterprise are not very high unless its managing director endeavours to understand the trade cycle and takes steps which avoid its worst effects. In fact, he has a moral obligation to his employees, his creditors and his shareholders to see that the firm is not defeated.

The trade cycle is caused by the very freedom of choice

which customers enjoy. If that freedom is worth preserving, then every effort must be made to achieve a thorough understanding of why industry suffers from ups and downs in the level of its activity. Every product or service of a durable nature, whose purchase can be postponed for one reason or another, is liable to suffer from a trade cycle. This means that in a country with a high standard of living, where people are well above the bread-line and where the purchase of most goods and services can therefore be postponed, nearly every product or service is subject to periodic swings in the total volume of sales.

One of the more obvious industries to use as an example in discussing the trade cycle is house-building, for every house-owner has some experience of it. If a typical house lasts for fifty years before it is condemned as uninhabitable, then in order to maintain the present stock of good houses, it would be necessary to build an average number each year equal to 2 per cent of the total stock. For example, if the total number of houses in a country is 10 million, this means building 200,000 houses a year just to maintain the existing stock.

Suppose that the population begins to grow and the standard of living rises. On both these counts the demand for houses may increase. To meet the additional demand it may be necessary to add another 2 per cent per annum to the stock of houses, making a 4 per cent increase altogether, so that the nation as a whole needs 400,000 houses to be built. To achieve this level of construction would mean a rise of 100 per cent in the rate of house-building above the 200,000 a year necessary for mere replacement of old houses.

Let us now look at the other side of the coin. People may decide to have fewer children or even to use less house-room, perhaps because they want to spend more of their money on travel, or there may be a shortage of finance for housing because people are diverting their savings to other investments.

The total demand for house-room may drop quite quickly

from 4 per cent to 2 per cent of the stock of houses. This does not appear to be a large drop, but it means that the number of new houses needed in a year falls from 400,000 to 200,000. This is a drop of 50 per cent in the demand for new houses.

Thus we see that there is a multiplier effect between the demand for house-room and the demand for houses. A mere drop of 2 per cent in the *total* demand for house-room means a 50 per cent drop in the demand for *new* houses. So at least half the building firms could face the risk of bankruptcy and half the employees in the building industry could become liable to unemployment!

Sharp falls and rises in the demand for houses tend to follow each other alternatively because a sudden movement in either direction tends to be self-reversing after a time. For example, if the industry did reduce its output of houses for any of the reasons given above, there would in time be a shortage of houses, so the demand for new houses would rise again. The increase in building activity which followed could, in due course, result in a surplus of houses, so there would then be a drop in demand, and so on, in a continuing cycle of ups and downs.

The extreme durability of most structures makes the building industry particularly prone to severe trade cycles. Any industry with a less durable product is likely to have less severe changes in fortune. However, we have already indicated that durability is not the only factor causing the trade cycle.

Even the packaged holiday industry has ups and downs, in spite of the fact that the 'product' is consumed immediately. It is, however, a postponable product. Large numbers of people may, for quite good reasons, such as uncertain exchange rates, decide to postpone or abandon their holidays, as they did in Britain in 1974, with the result that some holiday companies went bankrupt.

There are certain steps which can be taken by public authorities to alleviate a trade cycle. For example, in the building industry attempts can be made to smooth out the supply of housing finance so that it is neither greatly excessive one year nor very short the next. Nevertheless, a managing director cannot rely on the government to bale him out over the trade cycle. Indeed, well-intentioned government action, taken at the wrong time, may make the trade cycle worse.

It is very important, therefore, that an MD should take his own action to defeat the worst effects of an economic downturn. This involves first of all being regularly primed with good trade information. He needs to study the published statistics and also to keep his ear to the ground informally to hear how his industry is trading. His own firm's achievements and failures are not necessarily a guide; there may be special reasons why it is doing better or worse than average.

It is not enough for him to study trade figures of the recent past. He must try to project the future. The sort of questions to which he must seek answers are as follows: How often is there a downturn in the industry? When is the next downturn likely to begin? How severe is it likely to be, in terms of percentage change from peak to trough? How quickly does the drop in activity usually occur? What is the industry's recent history of survival and disaster among large and small firms? What are the key solvency ratios for firms in the industry? What are the limit figures for these ratios which should not be exceeded unless there is some special form of reserve backing for the company's capital?

A company's auditors and its bank manager will be only too happy to discuss limit figures for key ratios. The industry's trade association may also have information on the generally agreed safe levels for key ratios and it may have some special statistics on the industry's performance.

All trade figures, however, do need to be treated with caution. It is quite common for different sectors of an industry to have different trade cycles. In the example already given, the house-building sector of the construction industry is likely to have a different cycle from the office-building sector. This can help a firm which is big enough and versatile enough to move some of its activity across from one sector to another, but it will mislead a firm which studies only the figures for the total industry and which is heavily concentrated in one sector.

Having done his best to ensure that he is primed with good trade information, a managing director must be particularly careful not to stretch his company's finances by starting major new projects, either for the launching of new products or for the expansion of company facilities, just when the downturn of the trade cycle is beginning. The quickest way to bankruptcy is to be financially over-extended at this time.

His efforts to ensure that the firm survives a downturn and retains as many employees as possible, ready to make a quick recovery when trade improves, are an important social responsibility. He cannot expect, however, to discharge it well unless there is some government aid. He is entitled to expect aid, for the individual firm must trim its activities in accord with the trade cycle, but government can take the opposite tack. It can deliberately spend more money during a downturn and deliberately spend less during an upturn, thus helping to smooth out the peaks and troughs.

As there are many different industries in different phases of the trade cycle at any one time, hopefully the overall effect of government action will be neutral, so that we have a smooth-running economy.

Unfortunately, hope has not yet been fully justified by experience and there are a number of reasons why this is so. Firstly, it is not yet easy to discern when the trade cycle for any industry is beginning to turn down, let alone persuade the government to act immediately. Secondly, the ups and downs of an industry can easily be confused with a long-term trend. For example, when horse-drawn carriages were gradually being replaced by motor cars, at what point of time could one say with conviction that the depression in the carriage trade was not a temporary phase of the trade cycle but rather part of a long-term trend towards using less carriages? If the trade cycle cannot easily be distinguished from a long-term trend, it is not easy for a government to spend money in countering the effects of the cycle, without being accused of wasting public money. If, for example, when there was a sudden and drastic decline in orders for machine tools, the government were to try to help by ordering a large quantity of tools and putting them into stock, by the time the industry had recovered, some of the tools which had been ordered during the decline might be out-of-date and unsaleable except for scrap. Thirdly, the ups and downs of all the trade cycles in a country and the effects of government action may not result in a smooth-running economy. The total effect may be a cycle of rising and falling economic activity, like the 'beat frequency' which one hears when two aircraft engines are not perfectly synchronised.

When a government tries to smooth out the ups and downs of the total economy, it needs to obtain a high degree of international co-operation on financial matters, for it must be able to alternate between spending less money and thereby increasing its currency reserves, and spending more money and thereby depleting its reserves. A moderately high degree of co-operation is, in fact, usually achieved. One of the lessons of history since the International Monetary Conference at Bretton Woods in 1945 is that civil servants and government ministers co-operate better when they are abroad than when they are at home. Even so, it is not easy to get the timing right for international co-operation.

The net effect of all the cyclical and long-term trends in industrial activity may be that particular regions of a country decline and others grow. Most governments today have regional development policies for aiding the areas of decline. These policies usually involve helping firms which set up business in these areas by the provision of free or cheap capital and by other forms of subsidy.

A managing director whose business is expanding must be continually on the lookout for opportunities to obtain free or cheap capital and other subsidies too. He should inquire what is available from the Department of Industry, the Department of Employment and from his own local authority.

If he takes advantage of any of the opportunities, he may find himself running a business on two sites many miles apart. This will bring new problems of travel and communication which may be regarded as a nuisance or a challenge, according to taste. Location on two sites should not be contemplated until the MD has a very good number two who is ready to be put in charge of the second site.

When government provides financial aid in various forms towards maintaining the level of economic activity, it is more concerned with the level of employment than with what happens to any particular company. Full employment policies since 1945 have aimed at maintaining the total level of private and government spending in the hope that this would result in the maintenance of a high level of employment. These policies have, however, resulted in continuing inflation. In 1945 Lord Keynes managed to gain international acceptance for a full employment policy as basic to co-operation between nations, but since the early 1970s his reputation has suffered from the criticisms of economists who argue that his policies were mistaken and that they must inevitably lead to inflation.

It is the author's view that the economic analysis of John Maynard Keynes was basically sound and that his full employment policy need not result in inflation. However, Keynes had never run a business other than a personally operated investment business. His writings reveal a lack of understanding of the relationship between capital and labour and the effect that this might have on his policy.

No managing director need suffer from this particular misunderstanding for he is working with labour and representing capital every day. However, we must wait until the sequence of arguments and facts in this book has unfolded as far as Chapter 16 before it is possible to set out the reason why the author considers that a managing director can believe in the possibility of having full employment without inflation.

11

Techniques of Capital Accumulation

HOW SUCCESSFUL FIRMS GROW

In Chapter 2 we proclaimed without apology that a managing director needs to be strongly motivated by money in order to be successful at his job. This usually means that he wants both a high income and the opportunity to accumulate personal capital. He dreams of being rich, if he is not already so. His desire for personal capital is natural; if his business is successful, it will generate capital for the shareholders. He will want to be a shareholder and to participate in the capital accumulation which takes place in a successful business.

What are the basic techniques by which successful businesses generate large amounts of capital, in spite of high tax rates? How is it that some people, starting from scratch, become millionaires in five, ten or fifteen years, in spite of all the difficulties and discouragements created by the government? In particular, how is this done legitimately—with new examples of the 'rags to riches' story being blazoned forth in the media every week or so?

There are two distinct parts to this process of capital accumulation. First is the problem of creating a large stream of business income. This is something which can be worked at and planned for, but not anticipated. Many are called but few are chosen. A company can budget for an increase in sales and try hard with a new product. Each aspect of customer appeal can be endlessly discussed and decisions made with the aim of doing the best on behalf of its customers, within the limits of acceptable costs. Yet at the end of the day they will individually decide whether or not to buy.

In most cases, the customers will simply continue with their old buying habits, unexcited by the new product on which so much care and attention have been lavished. If the managing director is lucky, they will try his new product and give it a cautious vote of acceptance. If he is unlucky, they will buy so little of it that he must quickly abandon the new venture before it ruins his whole business. In rare cases, the new product will be accepted with such enthusiasm that its sales figures soar skywards and cause a dramatic leap in profits. The sudden escalation of demand for a product is so rare that it is unlikely to happen to most businessmen in the whole of their lives. When it does happen, the multiplier effect on profits can be exceedingly high.

This phenomenon of the occasional escalation of demand is seen in many industries. An obvious example is in the pop music industry, where most pop groups have average success, but where occasionally one particular group becomes exceedingly popular. It is seen in the retail industry, where most shopkeepers do only a modest trade, but where occasionally one is so successful that he quickly builds up a multiple chain of shops. It is seen in manufacturing, where most of the new products are failures and some have average success, but where occasionally one product lifts off to a level of demand which is beyond the wildest dreams of those who developed it. Ten case examples of different types of fast business growth are presented in Appendix I.

Why is it that an escalated demand can cause an enormous growth in the profitability of a business? A simple example will suffice. Suppose a product is costed and priced with a view to making a profit of 20 per cent on sales revenue when the number of units sold is 100,000, this 20 per cent being necessary to service the capital used in the business. If the product actually catches on and quickly sells 1 million units, the profit margin may rise to 40 per cent or more. Unit costs have fallen because of the larger quantities produced, but perhaps even more significant, if public demand for the product rises sharply as a result of verbal recommendation from one customer to another, it may be possible to cut advertising expenditure. So, at a time when demand for the product has multiplied tenfold, profit may be multiplied twentyfold. Although this is a rare event, the thought that some day it might happen keeps many a managing director working late into the night.

The second part of the capital accumulation process is concerned with what happens when a company has been lucky enough or skilful enough to establish a large stream of net income. How can this be turned into capital without too much interference from the tax authorities? Indeed, why can we be so confident that the tax authorities will not interfere with the process by which successful businessmen generate capital inside the business? The answer lies in the fact that the taxman is afraid of drying up the main source of business capital investment in the country and creating a drastic rise in the number of unemployed.

In the nation as a whole, the investments made by successful firms are partly counterbalanced by the disinvestments of unsuccessful firms which are losing money. Only the net figures, after deducting the losses from the gains, are seen in the national accounts. Any serious attempt by the tax authorities to interfere with the investment processes of the successful firm could quickly put the economy into decline. Here is an example. Suppose, for simplicity, that a country had only twenty business firms, each initially of the same size, and that ten were increasing their capital by 15 per cent per annum and that the other ten were suffering a loss, or capital decrease, of 10 per cent per annum. Net average capital growth in business firms in these circumstances would be $\frac{150-100}{20} = 2\frac{1}{2}$ per cent per annum. If, however, the government was to prevent the growth of the successful firms, net average capital growth would be $\frac{-100}{20} = -5$ per cent per annum. So, the national stock of business capital would decline by 5 per cent per annum and an ever-increasing number of people would be jobless.

What are the processes of investment with which the tax authorities dare not interfere? They are processes of business growth which are tax-allowable in most countries. In some cases, they are even subsidised by way of a special investment grant. Here are examples:

1 At the end of World War II, a young man came out of the services and used his gratuity of a few hundred pounds to set up a radio shop in the West of England. He made very good profits in his first year of, say, £10,000, but about £9,000 of this profit was used to set up other shops, so he paid tax on only £1,000. After ten years, he had a chain of 200 shops which he sold to a big group for £6 million. The reason he was paid such a large sum was that when he stopped incurring the costs of rapid growth, he had a profit of £10,000 on each shop, or £2 million in all, for 200 shops. The capital value of a private business with profits of £2 million per annum could easily be three times the profits, or £6 million.

2 Not far from the shopkeeper's home town was a family cider-making firm. They developed a new drink which was particularly attractive to young women. With the aid of a first-class advertising agency, they promoted it nationally with great success. All the costs of development and promotion were inevitably allowable for tax, and the firm's profitability grew so rapidly that it was able to go public and obtain a Stock Exchange listing. Then, by a reverse take-over bid, the family shareholders, who were now millionaires, were able to amalgamate their business with a large brewing group in which they became major shareholders.

3 A very successful manufacturing company found that, due to rapid expansion, its old-fashioned premises near the

115

centre of a city became very cramped. The board of directors decided to relocate in a development area in the north of Britain and to take advantage of all the various grants and allowances available. A magnificent new factory, warehouse and office block were built, equipped with the latest machines and facilities. The total cost was £16 million, of which somewhat over £4 million had to be found by the shareholders out of the company's profits. The balance was provided by national and local government authorities in various forms of subsidy, grant and tax allowance. Thus, the capital value of the business was greatly enhanced at public expense because the business was successful and could bring employment to a development area.

4 Whether a company invests in a development area or not, virtually all of its new plant and equipment is immediately allowable (in Britain) as a cost, for corporation tax purposes. Research and development expenditure can also be written off very rapidly. Thus, the successful company can expand by the reinvestment of profits in the business, paying little or no corporation tax. Add to this the allowances for appreciation in the value of stocks arising from inflation, and some fast-growing companies can be assured of accumulating capital out of profits which will not bear any major tax charge for years ahead.

In countries where stock-market activities are considerable and are widely believed to play an important part in industrial financing, the examples of capital accumulation which receive publicity are usually companies which have grown rapidly and are now about to go public and obtain a listing for their shares. The Stock Exchange prides itself in being an institution where ordinary citizens can invest their savings and so the impression is left that the successful businessman who floats his company on the Stock Market has somehow accumulated all his capital by personal saving out of income.

By contrast, the author has found that in those countries

116

of Western Europe where stock-market activity plays a much smaller part in industrial financing, the processes of business capital accumulation are seen more clearly for what they are: the building of a large stream of net income by a successful business and the conversion of this income into its equivalent value as capital.

This continental view is also valid for Britain, according to evidence presented in the author's paper entitled *The Changing Pattern of Personal Savings and Investment in the United Kingdom*, prepared for the Bournemouth Conference of the British/North American Committee, June 1976, and published in extract form in *The Times*, London, 26 August 1976. The table in Figure 14 summarises this paper and shows that the greatest generator of capital today is the successful business enterprise. By contrast, net personal savings are recorded as providing only 1.1 per cent of total British national capital over the ten-year period 1965–74.

Figure 14

BRITISH NATIONAL CAPITAL ACCUMULATION 1965–74

	per cent
Business organisations	52.5
Central and local government	22.9
Pension funds, insurance policies, mortgage repayments and hire purchase repayments	22.4
Non-profit organisations	1.1
Net personal voluntary saving	1.1
	100.0

An exaggerated idea of the role of personal saving in national capital formation comes down through more than 200 years of history from *The Wealth of Nations* by Adam Smith. He said:

. . . capitals are increased by parsimony, and diminished by prodigality and misconduct. Whatever a person saves from

117

his revenue he adds to his capital, and either employs it himself in maintaining an additional number of productive hands, or enables some other person to do so, by lending it to him for an interest, that is, for a share of the profits. As the capital of an individual can be increased only by what he saves from his annual revenue or his annual gains, so the capital of a society, which is the same with that of all the individuals who compose it, can be increased only in the same manner.

Parsimony, and not industry, is the immediate cause of the increase of capital. Industry, indeed, provides the subject which parsimony accumulates. But whatever industry might acquire, if parsimony did not save and store up, the capital would never be greater.

Adam Smith would have been right if he had been describing what generally happens when a new business is started. Unless the owner of the business or one of his forbears accumulated personal capital and avoided spending it on personal consumption, the new business could never get started. However, once the business is under way, capital is accumulated in the business and the owner's livelihood depends on leaving much of it there. Indeed, tax law makes it very difficult for him to take it out without paying high rates of personal income tax, so the effect is the same as if the business owner received a large tax concession to encourage him to accumulate personal capital within the firm.

By contrast, his employees who have no shares in the business regard personal savings as domestic savings accumulated out of after-tax income to pay for a holiday or an expensive household item. Thus personal savings can have two meanings, but the business version of it is misleading. This is not important on the level of small-scale, personally owned businesses, but the idea that business capital accumulation is personal saving becomes more dangerous when it is repeated with reference to large-scale businesses where the shareholders are usually unconnected with the directors who make the investment decisions. As Figure 14 shows, very little of total national capital accumulation is genuine personal saving. The vast bulk of new capital arises from the investment decisions of people who are not personally denying themselves, or saving, when they make the decisions. They are managing directors, government officials, pension fund and insurance fund managers who are handling other people's money.

Most prominent in this group, in terms of quantity of capital accumulated, are the managing directors. They are in a unique position to contribute to national prosperity by running successful businesses which generate large amounts of capital and increase the stock of invested wealth. The typical MD is strongly motivated to accumulate capital himself by becoming a shareholder in the business, if he and his family do not already own it. This motivation is important to the prosperity of the whole nation, which benefits from the increasing stock of capital—as long as it is remembered that there are others working in the business who may also like to have some shares.

It is particularly important for the managing director to remember this if he and his family own the business. Tax legislation for close companies is so tight that it is very difficult for the successful businessman to take money out of the business and reap the rewards of his labours, unless he either pays the top rate of income tax or sells the business. Thus, many business owners succumb to the temptation to sell out to one of the giant firms. Industry becomes more concentrated and family businesses are destroyed.

There is, however, another alternative. Shares can be sold to a profit-sharing trust fund which uses its profit-share to buy shares on behalf of employees. This way the owner can get some capital out on a basis which is allowable for corporation tax relief and the business can retain its independence.

12

Living with Democracy

A managing director has the difficult task of reconciling the various interests of customers, employees, suppliers, the local community and the providers of capital. Sometimes these interests conflict. If the MD should be over-zealous in the furtherance of any one interest, he may create a situation which could lead to the disruption of the very services which his company aims to provide. For example, his determination to meet the needs of customers may lead to disputes with employees over what they consider to be unreasonable work schedules. This is a particularly relevant example, for we are concerned in this chapter with the fact that a managing director who is eagerly serving the needs of his customers may, at times, be tempted to exercise almost dictatorial leadership over his employees, but this may not be easily reconciled with the aspirations of his employees for democracy at the place of work.

One problem with the type of instant-decision leadership which is sometimes needed in a business emergency is that it is habit-forming. The employer who acquires the habit of giving peremptory orders and having them unquestioningly obeyed in a crisis may continue to behave in the same way in normal circumstances. As a consequence, he may acquire a new set of attitudes towards employees.

The difference in attitudes between those leaders who cannot

120

live with democracy and those who are quite happy to do so was presented with enduring realism by Professor Douglas McGregor of Massachusetts Institute of Technology in 1960 in his famous contrast between theory x and theory y, contained in his book *The Human Side of Enterprise*:

Theory x spells out the assumptions behind the traditional attitudes of coercive management, as follows:

1 The average human being has an inherent dislike of work and will avoid it if he can.
2 Because of this human characteristic of dislike of work, most people must be coerced, controlled, directed, threatened with punishment to get them to put forth adequate effort toward the achievement of organisational objectives.
3 The average human being prefers to be directed, wishes to avoid responsibility, has relatively little ambition, wants security above all.

Theory y spells out the assumptions behind modern participative management attitudes, as justified by the latest research into human behaviour and motivation:

1 The expenditure of physical and mental effort in work is as natural as play or rest.
2 External control and the threat of punishment are not the only means of bringing about effort toward organisational objectives. Man will exercise self-decision and self-control in the service of objectives to which he is committed.
3 Commitment to objectives is a function of the rewards associated with their achievement.
4 The average human being learns, under proper conditions, not only to accept but to seek responsibility.
5 The capacity to exercise a relatively high degree of imagination, ingenuity, and creativity in the solution of

organisational problems is widely, not narrowly, distributed in the population.

6 Under the conditions of modern industrial life, the intellectual potentialities of the average human being are only partially utilised.

Further light is thrown on the difference between theory x and theory y leaders by a study made by the Bavarian Ministry of Employment and Social Services in 1977. This involved asking 4,000 employees in 300 firms for their views on the characteristics of a good and a bad boss. Figure 15 gives the frequency with which those questioned gave certain types of answer.

Figure 15

CHARACTERISTICS OF A GOOD AND BAD BOSS

	Percentage Replies
Good Boss	
Discusses with the employee the best way to do his work	70
Acknowledges achievements	65
Is fair in his decisions	61
Fights for employees' interests	52
Knows his job well	44
Bad Boss	
Imposes his own decisions	61
Has an open ear for sneaks	60
Cannot treat anything confidentially	59
Is always interfering with the job	48
Takes no notice of suggestions	42
Has no sense of humour	31

A natural consequence of a managing director taking a theory x attitude to employees is that they want to combine to form an alternative centre of authority within the business in order to protect themselves against his dictatorial conduct. There is much evidence from history that it is difficult for them to combine effectively when the boss is antagonistic, unless they receive outside help from a trade union, which is wider in its membership than the number of employees of the firm itself.

The rise of trade unionism as an alternative source of authority in the business firm is worth looking at fairly closely to appreciate its strengths and weaknesses. The three main strengths are:

1 Because union membership is wider than the employee strength in the firm, outside help is available in a dispute with management. Perhaps the most important aspect of this outside aid, in day to day practice, lies in the amassing and comparison of rates of pay and working conditions. This gives the labour movement tactical strength. Instead of fighting futile battles founded in ignorance, the unions know when they are unlikely to settle for more money. They also know when to hold out for more.

2 Shop stewards within the firm have the backing of full-time officials who can, if need be, negotiate with management on their behalf. Employees usually prefer to have their own elected representatives negotiating for them and these negotiators should be able to look management squarely in the eye and say: 'There is nothing personal in this; we were merely elected to speak for the whole group.' Nevertheless, if a conflict becomes bitter, the employees' representatives can go anonymous by calling in outside officials to negotiate for them, with the result that management is no longer even speaking to their own employees—though the latter may be silent observers at the negotiations.

3 Employees can withdraw their labour and, at the same time, they can usually ensure that nobody else moves in to take their jobs. The ability to prevent others from moving in is derived from their links with employees in other firms. It is vital to the strength of the labour movement. The withdrawal of labour has very limited effect without it. This is what picketing, sit-ins and blacking are mainly about. They break up the free market in labour and give to the

123

present work-force an on-site monopoly. The existence of this monopoly calls for a completely different response from management from that which is relevant in firms where trade unionism is weak. A managing director can do harm to his business if, in this monopolistic situation, he persists in maintaining the traditional employer attitude to labour.

The basic analysis of wage policy made by Adam Smith over two centuries ago is still largely appropriate where firms are small and union power is weak. The employer treats labour as one of the bought-in costs of production, like materials, except that he hires labour instead of making an outright purchase. He does his hiring in the labour market at the lowest bargain price he can obtain. This helps him to keep prices down and thus to compete with other firms which are supplying similar products.

By contrast, when labour has monopoly power, it must be treated by management as a special kind of overhead cost which, nevertheless, contains an element of variable cost and which also contains variable capacity. A good analogy to this labour monopoly is the office building which a property company buys with the aid of a bank loan and lets to professional firms in small units. The property company's costs are largely overheads because of the interest bill on the loan and maintenance costs on the building, but a few costs, such as heating, may vary with the amount of space let. If the building is not fully let, further costs will be involved in letting the remaining space, but equally, more revenue will be obtained if it is let. The problem is to determine what is the best letting policy for the property company if it is to maximise its net revenue. Economic analysis gives us the basic principles for determining the right policy. It is not necessarily easy to put this policy into practice, but at least we know where we should be heading.

The situation is similar with a labour monopoly. Labour could, under the right conditions, use its capacity to produce more, or alternatively it could go slow without fear of removal and replacement. We know how to analyse the problem, and some possible solutions are discussed in the following two chapters. Again, it is not as easy to solve the problem as it is to state the principles involved, but effective payment systems can be designed for the labour monopoly situation and there are everyday examples of firms using them successfully. Indeed, the on-site labour monopoly situation is so well understood by economists of the Department of Employment in Britain that in 1977 self-financing productivity schemes which could cope with this situation were specifically excluded from the overall limits to pay increases laid down under phase 3 of the pay restraint policy.

We turn now to the weaknesses of trade unions as a source of alternative authority in the business firm:

1 A trade union produces nothing. It does not create employment or serve customers or create wealth, all of which a good management does. Therefore, the unions start with a handicap while business management starts with some advantages. Employees naturally want to support the business system of authority, if only to fulfil themselves and earn a high standard of living.

2 A trade union is a defensive organisation on behalf of its members and, as such, it must usually be organised democratically in order to represent them properly. Although a democratic system of electing representatives is clearly the right form of organisation for group defence of this kind, there is little evidence to support the idea that it is an appropriate form of organisation for creative work, involving the supply of goods and services to customers. Therefore, a union is bound to be limited in the basic satisfactions which it can provide for its members, except in a time of industrial crisis.

We should not underestimate a union's importance to members in a crisis, but a good management which can

125

minimise the need for a crisis can generally have a co-operative labour force. In fact, management can do more. It can promote active co-operation by the manner in which employees are consulted and also, as we shall see, by means of financial participation.

3 The trade union movement's ability to fulfil a positive role in industry has been weakened by the adherence of so many of its leaders to out-of-date political philosophies. These are perhaps best described as 'nineteenth-century blues', for, in the nineteenth century, trade unionism was almost entirely confined to 'blue collar' (ie, manual) workers. The political philosophies developed for them by well-meaning intellectuals were supported on twin pillars of wisdom. These were the concepts of equality and common ownership. Although these ideas have now lost much of their shine, it must be remembered that in the nineteenth century some 90 per cent of people lived in rented accommodation and had relatively few possessions. Manual workers, by middle-class standards, were large in number and relatively poor. In these circumstances, it was not altogether surprising that the needs of the individual should be largely ignored. Individualism was identified with the employers and the vast majority of employees had limited scope for giving vent to their individual tastes and attitudes.

A major aim of the working-class movement, devised for them by the intelligentsia of the middle class, was to capture the machinery of government in order to use it as a weapon with which to beat the employers, mainly by passing laws which protected labour. However, a logical consequence of capturing the government would be to use it to take over the capital resources of the 'enemy', ie, the employers. What would happen after the take-over, in the way of detailed organisation of industry, was not properly thought through; nor was enough consideration given to the effect of a continuing succession of such take-overs in putting more power in the hands of state officials and thus endangering human liberty.

Saddled with such philosophic aims, the trade union movement has made unnecessarily heavy going of the twentieth century, a period which has seen the steady growth of industrial automation. This has caused a continuing rise in the number of white-collar workers and a fall in the proportion of blue-collar workers until, in Britain, the white collars almost equal the blues, and in the United States and Germany the blues are already out-numbered.

White-collar workers generally live under quite different traditions and have different aspirations from those which were ascribed to blue-collar workers in the nineteenth century. White-collar people, on the whole, do not believe in equality because they tend to be career-minded. Each person strives for a self-fulfilling career of a kind which is suited to his capabilities and he expects to be paid at a rate which is appropriate for his particular job. In some cases, he may also expect merit awards on top of the standard rate for his job, payment of annual increments in recognition of the value of his experience, or the opportunity of promotion to a more responsible post on a higher level of pay.

Figure 16 shows a typical salary scale agreed between a white-collar union and a major company in London in 1977. Across the top of the table are the grades of authority and up the sides are the annual incremental steps. The two sets of bottom bars indicate the training area beyond which an employee cannot climb until he is judged to be of standard performance. After he has attained the standard level, he climbs one step a year as long as he is rated standard, until he reaches the bottom of the two upper bars; then he stops. If, however, he is rated superior in his performance, he climbs two steps a year and he can go on climbing up to the top bar. If he is promoted, he moves across to the next higher grade and begins in the step above his previous salary level. All this is far removed from the nineteenth-century cry for equality.

Figure 16
SALARY SCALE AND PERFORMANCE AWARD SYSTEM AGREED BY A WHITE-COLLAR UNION

£s annually

Grades	1	2	3	4	5	6	7	8	9	10	11	12	Steps
8	2640	2865	3090	3546	4092	4716	5418	6198	7056	8044	9058	10462	10
7	2540	2765	2990	3416	3936	4534	5210	5964	6796	7758	8746	10098	9
6	2440	2665	2890	3286	3780	4352	5002	5730	6536	7472	8434	9734	8
5	2340	2565	2790	3156	3624	4170	4794	5496	6276	7186	8122	9370	7
4	2240	2465	2690	3026	3468	3988	4586	5262	6016	6900	7810	9006	6
3	2140	2365	2590	2896	3312	3806	4378	5028	5756	6614	7498	8642	5
2	2040	2265	2490	2766	3156	3624	4170	4794	5496	6328	7186	8278	4
1	1940	2165	2390	2636	3000	3442	3962	4560	5236	6042	6874	7914	3
					2844	3260	3754	4326	4976	5756	6562	7550	2
										5470	6250	7186	1
Steps													Steps

The other nineteenth-century cry, for common ownership, has been badly mauled by popular practice. Suburbia has grown rapidly during the twentieth century and home ownership in Britain has risen from 10 per cent to over 50 per cent of all houses, owned mainly but not entirely by white-collar workers. Pride of possession has also extended rapidly in motor cars, boats and domestic durables from television sets to washing machines.

On the industrial front, the spread of ownership began in the United States of America in the 1950s and '60s with a boom in executive share option schemes. This was followed by a move towards general employee shareholding schemes, first with white-collar 'thrift plans' and then with deferred profit-sharing schemes for all employees. These latter schemes increased rapidly in number during the early 1970s, until there were over 200,000 companies with such schemes. In the twenty years up to the early 1970s, the experience of share ownership in the USA spread from 9 per cent to 25 per cent of the adult population, as estimated by the New York Stock Exchange. In recent years, a decline in the rate of share purchasing by individuals out of taxed income has probably been more than made up by the growth of ownership through company share schemes for employees.

In France and Germany special legislation also extended the scope for share ownership. As a consequence, the percentage of people of working age and above with shares rose from under 4 per cent in both countries to 9.2 per cent in France and 7.6 per cent in Germany, as estimated by the author.

Britain lagged behind and Professor E. Victor Morgan's 1975 survey of personal savings and wealth revealed that only 3.8 per cent of people of working age and above were direct owners of shares. The first report of the Royal Commission on the distribution of income and wealth revealed that in 1974 some 26.4 per cent of shares were owned by pension funds and life insurance long-term funds, on behalf of millions

129

of pension-fund members and life-policy holders. Though these are very important funds and have continued to increase rapidly in size, they have had negligible impact on people's feeling of ownership. They could have more impact, in the author's view, if accompanied by direct experience of share ownership.

In spite of Britain's backwardness on the industrial front, the craving for personal possession has shown itself in many fields and clearly it could not be bottled up by out-of-date philosophies. Farm ownership, for example, has changed radically. At the turn of the century, only 10 per cent of farm land was owned by the farmer himself, the rest being tenanted from big landlords. By the 1970s, over 50 per cent of farm land was owned by the farmer.

It does seem that a weak feature of the trade union movement in Britain is that many of its full-time officials and some of its key shop stewards are adherents of nineteenth-century philosophies which do not reflect the attitudes and aspirations of the fastest growing sections of union membership, and which may be increasingly questioned as to their relevance for the traditional membership. Many of the jobs which are still classified as manual involve substantial personal responsibility and a sophisticated combination of mental and physical skills. A straw in the wind to changing attitudes was revealed in a 1976 opinion poll in West Germany, showing that 61 per cent of the people classified themselves as middle class. Many of the people making this claim have highly paid jobs in the expanding borderline areas which involve a combination of mental and physical skills, such as in driving a juggernaut. It is quite clear from the population statistics for past years that a substantial majority of people participating in this survey must have been born into manual-worker families.

In spite of the publicity given to the leading members of the Trades Union Congress in Britain, union officials in general are finding that they are running not so much a mass movement as a small-group movement. Every section of every industry may, at some time, have a grievance and try to get it put right by industrial action. A strike by forty-six key transport drivers can hold up—and has held up—an entire industry for many days. At the same time as the reader may seethe with anger at the disruption and inconvenience caused by such small-group strikes, he may also admire the tolerance of a social system which not merely allows this to happen but which also goes to great lengths to protect and support the forty-six disrupters while they are fighting their case. They could be forty-six managing directors striking for the restoration of their net pay differentials; provided they were members of a recognised trade union, the labour movement would feel obliged to protect and support them.

In the 1970s there was a great increase in labour legislation, particularly relating to the settling of grievances and the protection of individual employee rights. This legislation may well prove to be the labour movement's greatest achievement, although it is surely incomplete in relation to the closed shop. Once a union gains a closed shop and has an absolute monopoly of the labour supply in some sector, the individual employee should be protected against the risk of expulsion from the union. If he has a duty to belong, then surely he must also be given the right to belong, otherwise he can be denied his livelihood simply by being expelled from his union.

A managing director ignores the labour legislation at his peril. He should know it in outline himself and someone on his staff should know it in detail, even if the firm is too small to have a personnel manager. There are plenty of simply written leaflets in this subject area, as well as the legislation itself.

It would be unfair to discuss the strengths and weaknesses of the labour movement without also discussing employers in the same terms. We have already referred to the great strength of the employers. They offer employment and the challenging opportunity to serve customers and create wealth at the same time. These are such strong cards that their problem of holding the support of employees is mainly a matter of getting rid of the bad cards from their hands. Many large- and medium-sized British companies hold the following three bad cards:

1 Lack of adequate incentive payment systems which could keep the rewards of the working team in line with increases in productivity and prices. As a consequence, employees are quite extraordinarily dependent on trade unions to fight the battle of fair pay. A wise company keeps one step ahead. It retains the loyalty of employees because it rewards them systematically and fairly before it is pushed into doing so. Chapters 13 and 14 examine some ways of doing this.

2 Lack of facilities for promoting employee share-ownership. As a consequence, 96 per cent of employees have no first-hand experience of the ownership side of industry. They know about labour but not about capital. They are excluded from half the system and they sometimes act accordingly. An example of the effects of exclusion on human behaviour is not easy to quantify in industry, but it can be seen in what happened to the Duke of Norfolk's housing estate on Sheffield Brightside. At the beginning of this century, this estate of workmen's terraced houses was built and let to tenants who mostly worked in the steel mills across the valley of the Don. Brightside is so called because it is the north bank of the Don, facing the winter sun, and it was therefore a desirable site for housing. At the time of writing this book, however, it could hardly be more dismal.

In the 1950s when some of the houses on Brightside were not much more than forty years old, the estate was condemned for slum clearance by the Sheffield City Corporation. However, most of the houses then remained, condemned but occupied, for another twenty years before the bulldozers moved in. Then rebuilding began, this time with council housing, but at a very slow pace. It is easy to condemn houses and pull them down, but it costs a lot of money to replace them.

132

At one end of the estate a small group of houses had earlier been allowed to come into the personal ownership of the people who occupied them. These few were spared from the bulldozers. It has cost relatively modest sums to modernise these houses and make them quite acceptable first-time homes for young couples. The cost of modernisation has been typically between one-seventh and one-tenth of the cost per house of pulling down the rest of the estate and replacing it with houses which are no bigger.

What really went wrong at Brightside? Why was it condemned so early in its life? The answer is plain. The people were largely excluded from personal ownership, the property they lived in was neglected and this process was made worse by rent control. Inevitably, therefore, the estate had to be demolished.

The law of human exclusion says quite simply: 'If you can't join 'em, beat 'em'. When people are excluded from property ownership, they are careless about it and may even destroy it. There are many examples like Brightside all over Britain. Carelessness towards property is most visible with housing. Carelessness with industrial property is more difficult to prove, because people are being paid to do a job of work. If they are careless, is it because they are bad at the job, or because they do not own a stake in the property? There are few available figures on the effect of property ownership on working attitudes, but those available are given in Appendix II. However, the wise managing director does not overlook the possibility that motivation may be improved if employees own a share in the company. The practical means of enabling them to do so are discussed in Chapter 16.

The law of human exclusion does not suggest that everyone must own shares before he is prepared to work well and look after property. It does not even mention property and not everyone wants to be an owner. The law is concerned with a matter of delicate social balance. If, in the

133

normal course of events, a substantial proportion of people become owners, then the climate of opinion is likely to be favourable to personal ownership and personal caring for property. If, at the other extreme—which is the case in Britain—over 96 per cent of the people have no direct shareholding in industry, then the prevailing climate of opinion is likely to be one of carelessness about industrial property and, in some circumstances, it may lead to obstructive action or even destruction.

3 Lack of consultative procedures for decision-making. Though some firms are good at joint consultation, many are poor. To be fair, one of the reasons why they are poor is the existence of an ideological gulf between the managing director's views about the nature of enterprise and how it can serve the community, and the views of his shop stewards on how the system should be changed in favour of State ownership and control.

One of the keys to effective consultation lies in the managing director's belief in a clear and forthright philosophy of enterprise which he is willing to expound and defend before any group of employees. Much of industry is on the run from politics and does not even answer back with an easy confidence, let alone assert a case.

Chapter 17 sets out a philosophy of enterprise, in summation of this book, which the author knows from experience can be used by a managing director to assert his ideological leadership. He can confidently do this to an extent which has rarely been seen in Britain for over 100 years.

Once this leadership is reasserted, there still remains the problem of ensuring that joint consultation actually takes place. Chapter 6 discussed the process by which at every level a boss should consult with his subordinates. To ensure that this is effective, it is advisable in a firm of any significant size to have a parallel line of communication via employee representatives. There needs to be an elected council in each major division, branch or subsidiary, which meets regularly with management. It should contain representatives of all levels and major groupings of employees. If some employees at the higher levels are reluctant to be represented, then they should be persuaded. It is the managing director's task to see that they are not by-passed in the communication chain.

An astute MD will make good use of his company's system of representative councils in two ways. First, the system may enable him to hear things which might not otherwise come to his notice through the direct chain of command. Secondly, it may enable him to put across his views and attitudes more effectively and further down the line than if he had to be reinterpreted by subordinates at each level of authority. In fact, there may be occasions when he will want to address the whole company of employees.

The period of service of elected representatives on employee councils should preferably be limited to no more than two years, followed by a period of ineligibility for re-election. By this means, a significant number of employees gain the opportunity, at some time in their working lives, to become an elected representative. Also, if the need for new representatives is kept fairly large in this way, those who are elected cannot too easily be labelled with one particular set of attitudes or identified with one narrow clique.

A managing director could not possibly attend all the works council meetings in a large organisation. If he has to delegate some of the attendances, it should be to members of operating management, not to a staff specialist such as an industrial relations manager. The main objective in every meeting should be to discuss the operating targets and results in a manner which all can understand, as described in Chapter 8. Grievances and problems should arise in the natural course of discussing the tasks in hand; they should hopefully never need to be the main items on the agenda.

At the pyramid of a joint consultative system one has to face the problem of whether or not there should be employee representation at board level. It is the author's opinion that, in the larger firm, where this subject is more likely to be considered, employee shareholding should take priority over the election of employees to the board. This order of priorities ensures that when board representation does occur, both the representatives and those who elect them have a double interest in the company and, accordingly, a better understanding of its prospects and problems.

It might be questioned whether employees have any more right to board representation than any other group of shareholders. In their capacity as shareholders perhaps not, but when their dual capacities are considered, their claim for representation, at least on a supervisory board, gathers more weight.

13

Motivation of the Individual

Do people generally object to others earning more money than they do? Apparently not. A survey conducted in Britain in 1977 by the Opinion Research Centre involved the interviewing of 1,000 employees about their attitudes towards pay differentials. The persons interviewed were carefully selected to represent accurately the different 'social classes' which are used for classifying people in surveys of this kind. Altogether 95 per cent of those in the survey thought that it was right to pay people more if they exercised more skill, carried more responsibility or had higher qualifications. The survey was conducted at a time when pay differentials had been eroded by the effects of inflation and when there were official curbs on increases in pay. Most people felt so strongly about the importance of differentials that they wanted them restored to their former levels.

The feeling in favour of pay differentials was strong in all social classes. Over three-quarters of manual workers thought that managers should be paid substantially more than shop-floor workers so that companies could attract good people to run the business. However, ignorance about the effects of taxation in reducing the spending money of the higher paid is apparently widespread. The people interviewed in the survey were more generous in their estimates of the net after-tax differentials which they thought the higher paid ought to

137

have than these senior people actually enjoyed. Figure 17 gives the net differentials after tax for each social class suggested by persons interviewed in the survey. The author's estimates of actual differentials after tax are given in the right-hand column. This column must inevitably contain some very rough figures because of the wide ranges of incomes applicable in the various job categories.

Figure 17
JUSTIFIABLE DIFFERENTIALS
(Expressed as a multiple of the unskilled manual worker level)

	After-tax differentials considered justifiable by employees interviewed in ORC survey	*Actual differentials after tax, as estimated by the author*
Unskilled workers	1	1
Skilled manual workers	1.25–2	1.05–1.50
Specially trained and qualified	1.50–3	1.20–2.00
Foremen and supervisors	1.50–4	1.30–2.00
Departmental managers	2–6	1.50–3.00
Senior managers	2.50–8	2.25–4.50
Managing directors and chief executives	5–10	4.00–9.00

It is the author's experience that differentials in pay within a working team are usually quite acceptable to the whole team provided that there is nothing underhand about them. To be fully accepted, they must be part of a pay structure which is openly known and which has a purpose that the managing director can describe and defend with easy confidence. One element in that purpose will be the need to recruit labour of the different types and skills necessary to fill all the jobs recognised in the firm's programme of work. There will be minimum levels of pay below which the firm may not be able to recruit labour. However, in some cases, these minimum levels may be below the rates paid by other firms in the district offering similar jobs.

The theories of labour developed by the classical economists in the late eighteenth and early nineteenth centuries suggested that there was a fairly perfect labour market in which employers and potential employees bargained finely over rates, keeping pay levels closely similar for the same type of job. If, as the author has reason to believe, Figure 18 is typical of modern industrial conditions, the situation is now very different from that in the time of the classical economists. Figure 18 is taken from the comparison sheet circulated regularly between the personnel managers of fifteen engineering companies in an English industrial town, comparing the weekly, or in some cases annual, earnings of a wide range of jobs up to and including foreman. To simplify the comparison, actual money rates of pay have been converted into percentages, taking for each job category the lowest earnings in that category and making it base, equal to 100.

All of these fifteen firms manage to fill virtually all vacancies, although the range in pay is typically from 100 per cent up to 150 or even 180 per cent. The lowest payers are not starved of labour. All the firms know what the others are paying and so do their employees. There is no market tendency to bring down the top earnings or bring up the bottom earnings. Firm A is clearly the high payer of the town. It fills vacancies easily but it could fill them at substantially lower rates of pay. Its high level of employee earnings arises from designing a payments structure for the purpose of motivating employees to produce high output, not for the purpose of recruiting them. A clear distinction needs to be drawn between minimum recruitment levels of pay and maximum motivational levels of pay.

The main element in the total purpose of a pay structure will be motivation. The structure must be designed to make clear to employees what they have to do to earn more pay—what greater skill, effort and responsibility they need to bear

139

Figure 18

BLANKTOWN DISTRICT SALARIES AND WAGES COMMITTEE ENGINEERING INDUSTRY

Bench Mark Earnings for November 1976

(Each firm is coded with a letter. For each job category the average earnings in each firm are expressed as a percentage of the average earnings for that job in the lowest-paying firm.)

	Firm A	Firm B	Firm C	Firm D	Firm E	Firm F	Firm G	Firm H	Firm I	Firm J	Firm K	Firm L	Firm M	Firm N	Firm O
Fitter maintenance	164.3	124.2	122.1	112.8	112.4	111.6	100.0	111.4	127.7	102.6	115.4	113.8	108.0	112.1	121.2
Fitter production	160.1	123.9	133.0	113.9	116.6	108.7	—	114.6	—	100.0	109.7	110.6	127.2	—	—
General labourer	150.9	126.5	116.2	104.1	100.0	112.6	103.7	111.4	128.9	107.0	116.2	108.6	108.1	108.0	120.6
Draughtsman	136.6	115.1	121.1	112.7	115.0	108.5	100.0	112.7	—	112.0	119.4	107.2	127.3	117.7	123.1
Clerical (20+) average lowest grade	145.5	112.8	110.9	133.8	100.0	124.1	112.6	117.5	155.3	103.7	122.7	120.0	121.6	123.4	131.8
Foreman lowest grade	160.6	140.5	100.0	147.7	138.3	166.7	—	142.1	186.4	155.2	156.4	137.8	147.2	143.5	161.4

and, in a few cases, what greater physical hardship, danger or discomfort may be required.

It has long been recognised that the main factors in determining pay differences are skill, effort and responsibility, with the addition in some cases of hardship, danger and discomfort. The problem is how to measure these factors in practice. It is a particularly complex problem because the system of measurement needs to vary from one part of the working team to another. For example, it is not easy to compare the hardship of a sales director who has to leave his family and go abroad for six weeks with the discomfort of a machine operator in a noisy part of a factory.

Fortunately, in designing a fair pay structure, we do not have to start from scratch. We can take a lesson from the work of King Henry II in the twelfth century. He was born in France but inherited the kingdom of England as well as most of northern and western France. He was a very capable man and he recognised England's need to have a common body of law which could be administered in his own royal courts, on a uniform basis, from one end of the land to the other. However, he was wise enough to realise that he did not have the ability to invent a completely new set of laws himself, so he sent law students on journeys throughout the land to discover what was already the accepted local law. For example, what was the penalty for stealing a sheep? Using all the information collected, Henry was able to compile the Common Law of England. This became a basic feature of the legal system now used in almost all the English-speaking countries.

Likewise, today, a managing director can start by compiling the average rates of a pay system. He can find out from his own files the current rates for various jobs. He can then supplement this knowledge with outside information, mainly from the relevant employers' association, if he is having difficulty in recruiting any particular types of labour. Where differentials have been eroded, he can either make adjustments himself or have a job evaluation exercise carried out.

Let us assume that the MD can then start with a situation of reasonable contentment about existing pay levels. This still does not add up to a pay policy, for he needs to have means of deciding when to make changes in pay levels and by how much. Moreover, to achieve maximum employee motivation he needs to make changes on his own initiative rather than to wait until he is pushed into doing so. In fact, he will be concerned with two types of change:

1 How the individual employee's pay changes in relation to other individuals, taking into account changes in skill, effort, responsibility, hardship, etc.
2 How the general level of team pay changes to take account of alterations in prices, productivity, and any other factors which are of common concern to the whole team.

The morale of a working team can suffer badly if a distinction is not made between these two types of change. Team co-operation is rendered very difficult if some members discover, as they will, that others have been able to bargain for pay improvements which include the common factors affecting all, such as price changes, but that not all members of the team have been included.

Therefore a primary need of a fair pay policy is to have a method of reassuring employees that they will maintain their differentials when the common factors affecting everybody are dealt with. We saw in Figure 16 on p 128 an example of a type of pay scale which can give this kind of reassurance to employees. Every level of pay for each job is set out on a grid and, from time to time, such as once a year, the whole grid is renegotiated with the relevant unions. Another way of achieving the same object is to have a points system, with every job given a points rating. In a small firm, this can be a simple system involving no outside, expert help.

The major advantage of having a points system is that when

there is more money available to spend on wages and salaries, it is only necessary to announce an alteration in the value of one point, and the employee knows that he has received his due share. For example, if an employee has 200 points and the value of a point goes up from £20 to £21, he knows that his pay has gone up from £4,000 to £4,200 per annum and that others have gone up in proportion. A points system for pay should preferably start at 100 points for the lowest paid full-time adult worker. Part-timers and juniors can then have their pay expressed as a percentage of 100. Also, higher-paid employees can see their own differential expressed as a simple percentage figure above 100.

The differentials between each job level on the co-ordinating hierarchy of a company should be a percentage which is acceptable to the industry. It will usually be between 20 and 30 per cent, measured in an upwards direction. This means that a person who is definitely in charge of several subordinates has a base pay of between 20 and 30 per cent above their general level. Many employees' jobs are not, however, a whole rank above or below the jobs of people with whom they work. The points system should allow for minor differences as well as for the bigger differences which recognise major jumps in responsibility.

Research into pay systems shows that the pay differences which people expect between levels of responsibility are similar, in percentage terms, all the way from bottom to top. For example, a production director expects to have the same margin of pay above his works manager as a foreman expects to have over his men. A consequence of this exponential relationship between pay levels is that we can easily calculate the top of a pay scale once we know the margin between levels and the number of levels. For example, if the acceptable difference between levels is 20 per cent and nine levels are necessary to co-ordinate all the functions of the firm, the ninth level will start at a salary which is 4.3 times the lowest level of full-time pay. If the acceptable difference between levels is 30 per cent, the ninth level will start at 8.16 times the lowest level. These facts can be checked in Figure 19. There is really no escaping the logic of a pay scale and no employee will seriously want to dispute it once he is given the opportunity to understand it. Therefore, the system is accepted more readily if it is openly available to all employees who are on the scale.

Figure 19

JOB BAND POINTS

	20 per cent Differentials		30 per cent Differentials	
	Bottom Line	Top Line	Bottom Line	Top Line
Ninth band	430	559	816	1,183
Eighth band	358	465	627	909
Seventh band	299	389	483	700
Sixth band	249	324	371	538
Fifth band	207	269	286	415
Fourth band	173	225	220	319
Third band	144	187	169	245
Second band	120	156	130	188
First band	100	130	100	145

Figure 19 gives the points ratings for the bottom and top lines of two salary band scales, one with 20 per cent differentials and the other with 30 per cent. Nine salary and wage bands are used in Figure 19 because this should be more than enough for most organisations, even those as large as the Post Office or General Motors. If the top man in an organisation has five subordinates, and if they in turn each have five subordinates all the way down the chain of authority, then nine levels will accomodate 488,281 employees.

The bottom and top lines of these scales are quite widely apart. As we have already seen in Figure 16 (p 128), relatively wide salary and wage bands provide scope within each band for recognising each person's length of experience and standard of performance, by the award of incremental points, on top of the basic points for the job. The wide bands may overlap, as indeed they do in Figure 19, with the result that an experienced employee in one band may earn more than a newly promoted member of the band above, although this situation may not continue for long if the overlap of bands is no more than the amount shown in Figure 19.

By contrast, the overlap of bands is much greater in the system shown in Figure 16. To make this clear, Figure 16 has been reproduced on a points rating basis in Figure 20 and the table has been turned around to appear in the same style as Figure 19, with the grades set out up the vertical columns.

It will be seen in Figure 20 that an employee who is not promoted but who moves through the incremental steps of grade 1 will, at the top of the grade, be earning more than someone in the middle of the next grade above. This type of system suits a white-collar union which must look after the member who is not promoted, but it also fits a general need of modern technology.

There are today many specialist areas, such as market research, scientific research, engineering design and advertising where a company does not want to promote all its best specialists beyond their level of managerial competence. The very able specialist may be needed as a specialist and not as a manager. Therefore, the salary scale should allow for considerable advancement within a specialist field, based on experience and performance, without the need for promotion to a managerial position.

The earnings progression system depicted in Figure 20 presents a neat compromise between the need for annual increments, which recognise the value of experience, and the need for merit awards, which recognise the value of actual performance. The compromise which has been adopted provides for annual increments which are automatic, as in the civil service, but it allows for two increments in the same year if an employee is rated superior in performance, instead of one increment for standard performance.

Figure 20

POINTS RATING OF SALARY SCALE

(Adapted from Figure 16 and made comparable with Figure 18)

Incremental Steps Within Each Grade

Job Grades	A	B	C	D	E	F	G	H	J	K
12	370	389	408	427	445	464	483	502	521	539
11	322	338	354	370	386	403	419	435	451	467
10	282	297	311	326	341	356	370	385	400	415
9	256	270	283	297	310	324	337	350	364	
8	223	235	247	259	271	283	295	307	319	
7	194	204	215	226	236	247	260	269	279	
6	168	177	187	196	206	215	224	234	243	
5	147	155	163	171	179	187	195	203	211	
4	136	143	149	156	163	169	176	183		
3	123	128	133	139	144	149	155	159		
2	112	117	122	127	132	137	143	148		
1	100	105	110	115	121	126	131	136		

This system of incremental steps is also suitable for coping with another problem. Occasionally, a company finds that it is having difficulty in recruiting people with a particular type of knowledge or skill; it may also be losing people of this type to competitors. There is a shortage of such people and so the generally acceptable level of pay rises above the company-structured rate. In such circumstances, it is a nuisance to revalue one particular job when it is uncertain how long or how severe the shortage will be. Figure 20 offers a way of alleviating this kind of shortage. If a company using this kind of scale finds that it can only recruit people in a particular job category by offering them a salary which is high up the steps of the grade to which the job has been allocated, this fact can be used as a warning signal that the company is in danger of losing staff in this job area. Consideration can then be given to awarding an additional annual increment of pay, on top of the one or two increments awarded for standard or superior performance, in order to bring up the pay level of competent members of the existing team so that it is more in line with that of the new recruits. If the shortage continues until most of the people in this job area have reached the top of their grade, the need for regrading the job can then be seriously considered.

An additional feature of the salary scale system depicted in Figure 20 is that it is inexpensive to administer and therefore particularly suitable to a small, independent firm or a subsidiary company which conducts its own salary administration. As we have already indicated, this type of scale minimises the need for expert job evaluation. Under the management/union agreement referred to on p 128, job grading is prepared by an eight-man management committee. Such a large committee is needed to ensure that the interests of all departments and functions are taken into consideration, that job responsibilities in one part of the business are not graded out of line with similar levels of responsibility elsewhere. However, the system of annual increments makes it unnecessary to have any precise determination of job points. Employees who are receiving increments are not generally worried about precise, relative levels of pay.

In deciding which grade a job fits into, management will be mainly concerned with the co-ordinating hierarchy of authority. Once the relationship of the job to others in the hierarchy is established, the precise salary of anyone occupying the job is determined by the fact that he normally starts at the bottom of his grade and moves up by increments. If, however, he has been promoted from a lower grade, he moves immediately to at least the salary step which is above his present salary. In some cases, his promotion may justify a higher move. The system is thus one of personal earnings progression based on career progress, determined by three factors:

1 Rate of promotion to higher grades.
2 Performance appraisal.
3 Increments which recognise experience.

A small firm adopting this type of salary grid can start with all the employees, including the managing director, relatively low down in the grading system. As the company expands and people take on greater responsibilities, they can be given new job titles and promoted to higher grades which automatically determine their salary levels. The main problem for the managing director will be to ensure that those who have to work together as close colleagues on a similar level of authority in the co-ordinating hierarchy are kept in the same grade, or at least in grades which are near to each other and which are above the grades of their subordinates.

The salary system illustrated in Figure 20 is a narrow-band system. Each grade is no more than about half a full band width. This is one reason for the extensive overlap of the grades. With this type of grading it is possible to accommodate a chargehand on a separate grade in between the foreman and his men. Typically, therefore, a boss will be at least two grades above his subordinates; some bosses will be more. For example, a finance director may be several grades above a member of his staff who is a fully qualified accountant but who has little experience of, and no responsibility for, departmental administration or for decisions on company finance.

How is the right grade for each employee actually determined? When a firm is small, the managing director can feel his way towards the right grade, watching both the rates of pay in the job market outside and the levels of skill, effort and responsibility, etc required for the job, relative to others. He will begin with a job description as outlined in Chapter 9.

For jobs relatively low in his co-ordinating hierarchy, he may find that his trade association has a suitable job evaluation system which is widely used in the trade. If the job is high up in the co-ordinating hierarchy, he may get by without a formal job evaluation system until his firm is fairly large, by which time he may want the advantages of one of the well known systems of management job evaluation on which guidance can be given by the relevant professional organisations —in Britain these are the Institute of Personnel Management and the British Institute of Management.

Most of the leading management consultants carry out job evaluations at the senior level. In the author's experience, the system for evaluating a job within the firm's structure and the parallel system for comparing it with similar jobs elsewhere and discovering the rates paid for it are both important, but they are much reduced in importance if the company has a pay system which covers every aspect of earnings progression.

What is meant by covering 'every aspect'? We have already indicated that an employee's personal earnings progression is affected by the following factors:

1 His rate of promotion to higher grades.
2 His performance appraisal.
3 His increments which recognise experience.

Earlier, we also discussed the need for adjusting all employees'. pay at the same time in recognition of certain common factors which effect pay. Therefore, we can now add to the above three factors an additional influence on earnings progression:

4 Changes in prices and productivity.

These four factors together recognise the need for both personal earnings progression and team earnings progression. They will now be considered individually in greater detail.

An employee's rate of promotion to higher grades will depend partly on the rate at which jobs in the higher grades are created through expansion of the business. Herein lies some of the explanation why fast-growing businesses usually have good industrial relations. Capable and ambitious employees have more opportunity for promotion and are therefore less likely to develop frustrations which they might possibly vent on the business.

An employee's rate of promotion is also, of course, affected by his personal suitability. This should be regularly assessed in his annual or biannual performance appraisal (see pp 95–6).

In the discussion of Figure 16 (see p 128), it was seen that a system of performance appraisal can be combined with a system of awarding annual increments of pay which recognise the value of experience. The method described was to award a single increment for standard performance and a double increment for superior performance, ie, for those receiving more than a specified number of marks. Also, a superior performer could rise further up the same grade, achieving additional increments beyond those available to a standard performer. There is much to recommend in this system. It is simple, and it accommodates the higher flyer as well as the standard performer, while both are within the same system and both are designated in salary by a simple code, such as 4F or 5H, indicating grade and step.

A company which thought that two criteria for appraising performance, standard and superior, were not enough could adapt the system for three criteria of appraisal—standard, above average and superior. In this case, instead of having a five-point difference between the steps of the lower grades, as in Figure 20 (see p 146), one could have a three-point difference and there would be about sixteen steps instead of ten. On an annual basis, a standard performer would move up one step, an above-average performer would move up two steps, and a superior performer would move up three steps. This system is illustrated in Figure 22 (see p 160).

It should be noted in Figure 20 that the number of points between steps in the same grade is virtually constant. This means that the percentage increase in pay achieved as an employee climbs the steps decreases slightly. It is a realistic arrangement which recognises 'the shape of the learning curve'. When a person enters a new job, his rate of learning is generally rapid at the beginning, but it slows down with the passage of time. Thus, an increment in pay which is intended to recognise the value of experience should be greater in the early stages of a new job and it should decrease in relative value with time.

The principle that there should be increments of pay which recognise the value of experience is perhaps most widely practised in the civil service. These annual increments have continued in the civil service during periods of pay freeze because civil servants were able to argue that they were 'self-financing'. What they meant was that the retirement of higher paid employees from the top end of the pay scale, to be replaced by lower paid people at the bottom end, balanced out the annual cost of the increments. If there were no increments, they said, the total level of civil service pay would actually fall. Therefore, the system of increments was self-financing and should be exempt from the pay freeze. At the end of Phase 2 of the pay policy in Britain in 1977, when new norms for increases in pay were established, self-financing schemes were specifically exempt.

A system of increments could, of course, exceed the self-balancing level and prove not to be self-financing. Research carried out for the Institute of Personnel Management by Mr George Mepham in 1976 showed that, in fact, public servants' pay as a whole had not been self-financing because many of the people recruited into local government had been recruited at the higher end of their incremental scales. Also, in the larger industrial companies it is generally recognised that an incremental scale system may involve a 'scale drift' of from 1 to 3 per cent per annum. We will see in due course how such a system can be contained within self-financing limits, but first we need to look at the wider use of the term 'self-financing' in industry.

151

14

Fair Pay for Employees

Because industry justifies its existence by whether or not customers continue to buy its products, the proper test of whether a pay policy is self-financing is if the company can afford it within the earnings currently obtained from its customers. Increases in wages and salaries should follow from improvements in prices and productivity. If, by contrast, the collective action of employees, through their unions, causes all the employers competing in the same industry to put up prices in order to recoup increased wage costs, such action is inflationary. As a result, the purchasing power of money is reduced.

If employees are to receive general increases in wages and salaries only when these can be accommodated within the increases in productivity which they achieve, and within the increases in prices which customers are willing to pay in a competitive situation, it seems reasonable that they should, in return, be guaranteed their share of such increases. It might be questioned whether an increase in earnings which arises from an increase in prices can ever lead to a fair share-out. Is this not just more inflation? The answer depends on who takes the lead. If the company's salesmen are able to persuade its customers that because of the good design of the products, or for other reasons, they ought to be content with paying higher prices, this is as much a measure of productivity gain

152

(eg, good design) as is an increase in physical output by shop-floor workers. On the other hand, if the lead comes from organised labour to push up wages regardless of productivity, the resulting increase in prices is inflationary.

The generally accepted way of determining whether there has been any increase in prices and productivity which the company can share with its employees is to measure the increase in value added. For this, however, we need a special way of looking at VA. The definition of value added which is relevant for value added tax is sales revenue minus the cost of bought-in materials and services. What we are looking at in this case is a direct tax system which avoids double-counting because the company deducts from its taxable sales revenue the cost of materials and services which it had to buy and which had probably already been taxed. What is left after making this deduction is the value added by the company and attributable to the services of capital and labour.

If the company buys a large quantity of raw materials all in one month, this cost can be deducted immediately for VAT purposes. It does not matter to the VAT man when the materials are consumed in the production process. He is collecting tax from a large number of firms and they are not all restocking their material bins in the same month, so for the tax-man the whole situation averages out.

It does matter to any one particular firm, however, when material costs are deducted. There is a false measure of value added if the costs deducted are greater, or less, than those of the materials actually used to make the goods sold during the month. As the proper cost figures are contained in the monthly management accounts, one is obliged to take figures of value added from these accounts. Hence, instead of deducting bought-in materials and services from sales, one just adds up, from the management accounts, the residual items of employee costs and trading profit before interest charges. It is first necessary, however, to allow for all new investment by depreciating it on an inflation-indexed basis and similarly to adjust stock usage for inflation, in order to arrive at a sum which is truly the value added by capital and labour together.

Research by Alan Rucker in America in the 1930s showed that over a forty-year period the share of value added which was taken by labour was fairly constant. It varied from one industry to another, as might be expected, but it was fairly constant within one industry from year to year. One possible explanation for this is that employers allowed themselves to be bidded up in wage bargaining, until labour had restored its traditional share of value added; the employers would then go no further. A good negotiator on the labour side would know when the limit had been reached.

If, at every bargaining time, employers do behave like this and concede to labour their traditional share of value added, it can be argued that they might as well concede it in advance, so that labour is virtually guaranteed its share. This way, employers gain goodwill and also establish a better prospect of achieving increases in productivity, since employees will know that they can automatically earn their share of any increases in productivity.

One problem in operating a value added pay system lies in determining the right employee share of value added. To do this, it is necessary to study the company's history of the ratio of employee costs to value added and also to study the history of the rate of return on capital employed, both in the company and in the industry.

Even when an appropriate ratio of employee costs to value added has been established, it is easy to fall into the trap of adopting a closed system by which one is perpetually trying to bring employee costs up to the right ratio of value added, without making adequate provision for future capital expenditure which could be important to the livelihood of every employee. If one is too generous to employees with immediate cash payments, one can in fact destroy their future jobs.

All value added systems effectively involve a high rate of profit-sharing, but only of the 'excess' profits above the previous average level. Therefore, it is sensible to adopt an open-ended system which aims to ensure that the right amount of profit in relation to employee costs is set aside before the 'excess' profit, which represents the increase in value added, is shared.

In principle, employees should receive their full, traditional share of the excess. However, an expanding company cannot afford to give out such a large amount of extra cash. It was one of the errors of the early Rucker enthusiasts that they did not appreciate this. In any case, a lower rate of cash bonus is quite adequate and very acceptable as a means of employee motivation.

The appropriate percentage to be shared in cash is a matter for judgement, but it is related to the ratio of employee costs to value added. As a result of work done by the author with Professor Peter Moore of the London Business School, it is now possible to develop a Bonus Grid which is specific to the circumstances of any particular firm and from which can be read the total level of bonus which the company can afford to pay, once its results for the immediate past period are known. Part of this bonus is available in immediate cash; part of the remainder may be carried forward against the possibility that there will be no bonus next time. Another part is available for investment in shares, on behalf of employees, via a deferred profit-sharing scheme. This money thus goes back into the business to help finance the investment programme. As can be seen from the example given in Figure 40 (p 248), the Bonus Grid relates the increase in value added, if any, to the profitability of the business and enables employees to see at a glance their shared interest with the company in maximising both profits and bonuses.

How can all the four factors in earnings progression be brought together in a non-inflationary, self-financing pay package? Each of the first three factors discussed—promotion to higher grades, performance appraisal and increments which recognise experience—may, in practice, be operated in a way which causes wage and salary drift and which therefore adds fuel to inflation. Overtime earnings and bonus payments to manual workers may also cause drift. However, the effect of drift can be neutralised when the fourth factor, changes in prices and productivity, is taken into account.

If we assume that the value added calculation results in a decision to raise employee pay by 5 per cent, and if a 1 per cent rise in employee costs has already taken place due to wage and salary drift, this is deducted first, so that there is only 4 per cent remaining to be added to employee costs to bring them back into the right relationship with value added. This entails making a 4 per cent adjustment to the value of one point on the wage and salary grid. Thus, a value added system can ensure that the pay system as a whole is completely self-financing even when there is drift in one or more of its parts.

An annual adjustment of wage and salary levels in recognition of an increase in value added may not appeal to employees in some industries which are accustomed to bonus payments. It is not, however, necessary to wait twelve months before providing a pay-off. The employees' cash share of the increase in value added can be paid as a monthly bonus. If this is done, it is generally sound policy to consolidate into basic wages and salaries half the average bonus rate every twelve months. As before, this entails adjusting the value of one point on the salary grid so that all wages and salaries rise by half the average bonus level.

In some cases, special categories of employees may prefer to stay on their own tailor-made bonus system. For example, direct and indirect production workers may already have a bonus system based on the physical output of the former. Sales managers and salesmen may already receive a commission on sales. Top management may already receive a share of profits. Such arrangements can be fitted in with a value added system. The special categories continue to receive their special bonuses, possibly at adjusted rates. They do not also receive the full VA bonus paid to other employees, but they might receive part of it and also the benefit of periodic consolidation of half the value added bonus into basic pay, so that their salaries and wages keep in step with those of the remainder of the working team.

We conclude this chapter by setting out, as guideline notes, the steps in establishing an earnings progression system which is completely self-financing and which therefore protects the company's financial resources while at the same time providing strong motivation for employees.

1 Draw up a wage and salary grid which lists the salary grades on the left-hand side and the steps within each grade across the top. Figure 21 (see p 158) presents a standard version of the special-case grid presented in Figure 20 (see p 146). The reader can vary the dimensions of Figure 20 to suit his own company's needs. For simplicity, Figure 21 depicts intervals of 10 per cent between grades. The intervals between steps on any grade are uniform in the number of points, beginning with five-point intervals on the bottom grade and adjusting periodically so that a 5 per cent value is restored in the higher grades. The five-point system is suited to performance appraisal which results in judgements of employee performance as being either standard or superior. If a three-way judgement is required, such as standard, above average and superior, a three-point system is better. This is depicted in Figure 22 (see p 160). As can be seen, it involves more steps, but some of these—for example, all beyond step L —may be reserved for those who achieve above average or superior appraisals. Thus, the last five steps provide opportunity for salary increases for the specially skilled who are expert in their subject but who either do not want or do not achieve promotion to higher grade responsibilities.

2 It may not be possible to put all groups of employees

Figure 21

WAGE AND SALARY GRID WITH INITIAL FIVE-POINT INCREMENTS AND WITH 10 PER CENT INTERVALS BETWEEN GRADES

Incremental Steps Within Grades

Wage and Salary Grades	A	B	C	D	E	F	G	H	J	K
25	970	1019	1068	1117	1166	1215	1264	1313	1362	1411
24	895	940	985	1030	1075	1120	1165	1210	1255	1300
23	814	855	896	937	978	1019	1060	1101	1142	1183
22	740	777	814	851	888	925	962	999	1036	1073
21	673	707	741	775	809	843	877	911	945	979
20	612	643	675	707	739	761	783	815	847	879
19	556	584	612	640	668	696	724	752	780	808
18	505	530	555	580	605	630	655	680	705	730
17	459	482	505	528	553	576	599	622	645	668
16	418	439	450	471	492	513	534	555	576	597
15	380	399	418	437	456	475	494	513	532	551
14	345	362	389	406	423	440	457	474	491	508
13	314	330	346	362	378	394	410	426	442	458
12	285	299	313	327	341	355	369	383	397	411
11	259	272	285	298	311	324	337	350	363	376
10	236	248	260	272	284	296	308	320	332	344
9	214	225	236	247	258	269	280	291	302	313
8	195	205	215	225	235	245	255	265	275	285
7	177	186	195	204	213	222	231	240	249	258
6	161	169	177	185	193	201	209	217	225	233
5	146	153	160	167	174	181	188	195	202	209
4	133	140	147	154	161	168	175	182	189	196
3	121	127	133	139	145	151	157	163	169	175
2	110	115	120	125	130	135	140	145	150	155
1	100	105	110	115	120	125	130	135	140	145

immediately on the wage and salary grid. Some unionised groups may wish to remain outside for the present time, but the grid should be available for them to join at an appropriate time in any year.

3 In transferring employees to the grid, one does not usually have to go to the expense of a complete new job-evaluation exercise. Unless the existing pay structure is badly out of line, much of it can be recognised as valid for direct transfer. This can be done at the time of year when employees' pay is being reviewed. They can be transferred direct to the grade and step equivalent to their new level of pay. Due to the overlap of grades, there will often be two or three grades and steps with the same or a similar number of points. In such cases, it is usually better to choose the highest grade. This provides the employee with more scope for incremental progression in the future. The decision will, however, depend on comparing the selected grades for people who ought to be on the same level.

4 Where differentials have been eroded, the transfer of employees to a wage and salary grid provides at least two opportunities for restoration of differentials. Firstly, job evaluation of the jobs with eroded differentials can be effected at the same time as the transfer so that the aggrieved employees start off at new levels of pay. Secondly, if it is not possible to completely restore differentials in one year, aggrieved individuals can be told that they will receive additional increments for each of the next few years until full restoration is effected.

5 When an employee is promoted, he moves at least into the next grade, to the salary step immediately above his recent salary level. Sometimes he may be promoted to a higher level than this.

6 Employees generally receive annual increments, moving up at least one step a year, except trainees in any grade who do not usually move beyond the second step until fully trained.

Figure 22

WAGE AND SALARY GRID WITH INITIAL THREE-POINT INCREMENTS AND WITH 10 PER CENT INTERVALS BETWEEN GRADES

Incremental Steps Within Grades

Wage and Salary Grades	A	B	C	D	E	F	G	H	J	K	L	M	N	P	R	S
25	970	999	1028	1057	1086	1115	1144	1173	1202	1231	1260	1289	1318	1347	1376	1405
24	895	922	949	976	1003	1030	1057	1084	1111	1138	1165	1192	1219	1246	1273	1302
23	814	838	862	886	910	934	958	982	1006	1030	1054	1078	1102	1126	1150	1174
22	740	762	784	806	828	850	872	894	916	938	960	982	1004	1026	1048	1070
21	673	693	713	733	753	773	793	813	833	853	873	893	913	933	953	973
20	612	630	648	666	684	702	720	738	756	774	792	810	828	846	864	882
19	556	573	590	607	624	641	658	675	692	709	726	743	760	777	794	811
18	505	520	535	550	565	580	595	610	625	640	655	670	685	700	715	730
17	459	473	487	501	515	529	543	557	571	585	609	623	637	651	665	679
16	418	431	444	457	470	483	496	509	522	535	548	561	574	587	600	613
15	380	391	402	413	424	435	446	457	468	479	490	501	512	523	534	545
14	345	355	365	375	385	395	405	415	425	435	445	455	465	475	485	495
13	314	323	332	341	350	359	368	377	386	395	404	413	422	431	440	449
12	285	294	303	312	321	330	339	348	357	366	375	384	393	402	411	420
11	259	267	275	283	291	299	307	315	323	331	339	347	355	363	371	379
10	236	243	250	257	264	271	278	285	292	299	306	313	320	327	334	341
9	214	220	226	232	238	244	250	256	262	268	274	280	286	292	298	304
8	195	201	207	213	219	225	231	237	243	249	255	261	267	273	279	285
7	177	182	187	192	197	202	207	212	217	222	227	232	237	242	247	252
6	161	166	171	176	181	186	191	196	201	206	211	216	221	226	231	236
5	146	150	154	158	162	166	170	174	178	182	186	190	194	198	202	206
4	133	137	141	145	149	153	157	161	165	169	173	177	181	185	189	193
3	121	125	129	133	137	141	145	149	153	157	161	165	169	173	177	181
2	110	113	116	119	122	125	128	131	134	137	140	143	146	149	152	155
1	100	103	106	109	112	115	118	121	124	127	130	133	136	139	142	145

7 Those who receive a standard performance appraisal move up one step a year until they reach the top limit for standard performers. If the salary grid is like Figure 21, those who receive a superior performance appraisal move up two steps in that year. If the salary grid is similar to Figure 22, those who receive an above average performance appraisal move up two steps in that year and those who receive a superior performance appraisal move up three steps.

8 The salary grid system can be run in conjunction with a value added bonus system. A ratio of employee costs to value added is agreed and used to determine the employees' share in any increase in value added. When value added rises, employees receive their share of the rise as a monthly cash bonus. A Bonus Grid may be used to relate the size of employee bonus, as a percentage of pay, to both the increase in value added and the profitability of the business. Employees already receiving special bonuses suited to the nature of their work usually receive only part of the value added bonus.

9 At the end of the year, half the average rate of value added bonus is available for consolidation into employee pay. Consolidation is effected by adjusting the value of one point on the salary grid so that everybody's pay is adjusted together. However, in case there has been any drift in the grid system arising from an excessive amount of upgrading or over-generous performance appraisal, for example, the total level of employee costs is reassessed after performance appraisals have been completed. Any drift in the system is deducted before bonus is consolidated into pay.

10 In cases where cash bonuses are not suited to a company's need, it may be appropriate to effect a direct raising of wages and salaries quarterly or half-yearly in step with rising value added. In such cases, it is particularly important to raise employee costs by only a proportion of the

increase in value added, keeping something in hand in case of a subsequent fall so that if such a fall takes place wages and salaries need not be reduced in proportion.

11 Whenever the value of one point is changed, and after this has been explained to and discussed with employee representatives, the wage and salary grid is converted from its points basis into a scale similar to Figure 16 on which each employee can directly read off the new level of pay for his grade and step.

12 Figures 21–2 have been extended up to grade 25 so that readers can assess, for the size of their firm, appropriate levels of top management pay. The full scale, up to the top level which the company needs, should be available for discussion with employee representatives, but there is no point in publishing top management's pay levels. They can work out for themselves what their salaries should be.

Finally, it may be said that a self-financing pay package which includes both personal earnings progression and team earnings progression has the following advantages:

1 It is non-inflationary and therefore likely, on past precedent, to escape from future periods of pay restraint.

2 It limits the company's commitments to levels of pay which it can afford, as measured by the increase in value added.

3 It unites the team of employees in seeking to improve productivity, from which they all gain.

4 It allows for special bonus systems to be taken into the overall system.

5 It reassures employees that their pay will rise in line with prices, in so far as the company is able to raise prices to its customers.

6 It provides a system of annual increments for employees in recognition of the value of their experience to the company.

7 It accommodates the particular needs of professionally and

162

technically qualified employees, some of whom may have to remain as specialists rather than accepting promotion to higher managerial positions.

8 It also accommodates a system of performance appraisal which encourages improvement in employees' performance, assesses them for promotability and regulates the rate at which they move up the steps of their grade.

9 It minimises the need for formal job evaluation in the smaller firm and it can be fitted in with any existing system of job evaluation in the larger firm.

10 It helps to answer the perennial question when making a new staff appointment: 'What can we pay him?'. After the annual review of salaries, if a list of managerial and professional employees, showing the grade and step of each, is circulated to key managers, it becomes somewhat easier to perform the difficult task of slotting a new employee into the pay structure. The consequences of getting him into the wrong pay relationship with his new colleagues are quickly apparent.

15

Rewards for the Top

ACCEPTABLE SALARY SCALES AND BONUS SYSTEMS

We saw from Figure 19 on p 144 that an organisation with nine full salary bands and a pay differential between bands of 20 per cent has a top level of pay averaging about five times the bottom level. If the pay differential between bands is 30 per cent, the top level of pay averages about ten times the bottom level. In Western Europe generally, top levels of pay are between five and ten times the bottom levels.

A managing director's salary level is clear enough. He is at the top of a co-ordinating system of salary levels, each requiring a differential large enough to be acceptable to a person promoted to a superior position and small enough to be acceptable to his subordinates. Motivation to seek and to stay in top jobs is provided very simply in this way, so long as tax rates are not too high. This important proviso will be discussed at the end of this chapter, after an examination of the three other elements in top management reward—cash profit-sharing, capital accumulation and fringe benefits.

As we indicated in Chapter 14, top management is one of the special categories of employee to whom it may be worthwhile paying a cash bonus based on performance. The relevant measure of performance for top management is the company's profitability, for the decisions and actions of the managing director and some of his immediate subordinates can significantly affect profits.

The formula for profit-sharing cannot generally be simple. If, for example, it was decided merely to take 2 per cent of profits and divide this among top management, the company could be storing up trouble for itself. Such a simple formula would mean that top management could receive a profit-sharing bonus even when profits were inadequate to provide shareholders with the equivalent of bank interest on their investment. It would also mean that if the number of participants in the bonus could be restricted, on the simple basis of not taking into the scheme new managers who were replacing those who retired or left, then it would be possible for the remaining participants to build up a situation where they were receiving extremely large bonuses in relation to their salaries. Finally, such a simple system could create an inducement for managers to push as much revenue, and therefore profit, into the immediate financial year, regardless of whether this was best for the company. On all these grounds the profit-sharing formula, to be effective, cannot avoid having some complexity.

1 Allowance should be made for shareholders to earn a reasonable return on their capital before sharing the balance of profits with management. This reasonable return might be 20 or even 30 per cent in a country where inflation is rapid, interest rates are high and corporation tax is 50 per cent or more. Alternatively, the reasonable minimum might be based on a value added formula, as described in Chapter 14.

2 The excess rate of return on capital employed, above the reasonable minimum, should be linked to a bonus based on the manager's pay. There might, for example, be a one-for-one linkage. In this case, for every 1 per cent of profit earned on capital employed above the reasonable minimum, the manager would receive a profit-sharing bonus of 1 per cent of salary. On the other hand, the appropriate linkage might be two-for-one or one-for-two or some other ratio.

This would depend on the nature of the industry and the circumstances of the firm.

3 The reasonable return expected by shareholders on the balance-sheet value of capital employed would depend on how up-to-date the balance-sheet was in its valuations. If these valuations were up-to-date, the return expected could be lower than if the valuations were out-of-date, after a period of inflation.

4 There should generally be a limit, expressed as a percentage of salary—such as 30 per cent—on the size of a cash profit-sharing bonus which can be paid in any one year. Any surplus entitlement should be carried forward to the next year. This process of carry-forward has two advantages. It provides for the possibility that next year may be a poor year financially and it also discourages managers from 'milking' one year at the expense of the next. It therefore adds to the sense of business continuity among the management team.

Schemes for capital accumulation by managers are also concerned with continuity. The closer a manager is to the top of a business, the more aware he becomes that his decisions and actions can directly affect the profitability of the company and hence the value of its shares. If he and his family do not already own the business, but nevertheless he is successful at running it, he begins to think in terms of the desirability of setting up a similar business on his own, so that he may accumulate capital in the same way as the present owners. However, he may not have the necessary initial capital for setting up.

In these circumstances, the next best thing for him to do is to acquire a financial stake in the firm where he is working. There are broadly two ways of doing this. The first method is for the manager to be granted an option on shares at their current value. The advantage of this method is that he need not exercise the option if the value of the shares does not rise

166

above what they were worth when the option was granted. If it does rise, then by exercising the option he acquires shares at a value below the price at which he can sell them, so he has an immediate potential gain which he may subsequently realise by selling the shares.

The second method is via deferred profit-sharing. A small percentage of the profits is used to subscribe for shares for managers and these shares are not immediately saleable. In later years when they can be sold the manager may make some personal capital, provided that meanwhile the shares have not fallen drastically in value. They may, of course, have risen in value, in which case the manager could accumulate substantial capital, subject to taxation being moderate.

Unless taxes were very low indeed, he could not, of course, do as well financially as if he were the majority owner of the business and had accumulated a large amount of capital in the business, using one or more of the techniques of capital accumulation described on pp 112–19. If he was resident in Britain, a successful business owner who built up a valuable business would be due to pay capital gains tax at 30 per cent on his gains from the sale. He might be prudent enough to change his country of residence before finalising the sale—as many people have done—he could move to a territory not far offshore where there was no capital gains tax.

In spite of the tax penalties for managers, by comparison with independent business owners, deferred profit-sharing schemes are worthwhile and they have certain advantages over options:

1 The money used to subscribe for shares is allowable for corporation tax, so the company has the use of reinvestment funds on a tax-allowable basis.
2 This method is particularly useful in public companies with operating subsidiaries. The managers of subsidiary companies may be awarded a deferred bonus which is based at least partly on the profits of each subsidiary, but it may be

appropriate for the bonus to be used in subscribing for shares of the group company on behalf of the subsidiary company managers. Thus, each manager is given an interest in both his own operating company and the total group.

3 A deferred profit-sharing scheme for managers ties in well with a similar scheme for general employees. We will discuss this further in the next chapter, but here it is relevant to say that general employees do not make the day to day decisions which affect company results in the way that managers do, so it is usual for a general scheme to involve profit-sharing at group level rather than at the subsidiary-company level. All employees with a specified minimum period of service, including managers, should belong to the general scheme. Separately, however, managers may participate in another scheme which, as described in the previous paragraph, gives them a share in those profits of their own subsidiary which exceed a minimum rate of return on capital employed. This may be basically a cash profit-sharing scheme, with a ceiling which is expressed as a percentage of salary and with provision for carrying forward any surplus to the next year. If such a surplus is not needed in the next year to make up the basic cash bonus, it may provide a convenient source of funds for managerial capital accumulation. In this event, it is not seen as an additional perk for managers, but as part of an incentive profit-sharing bonus to which they are entitled by the nature of their job, in the same way that a salesman may earn commission and a direct production worker may earn an output bonus.

The word 'perk' became fashionable in the 1960s as a political weapon for attacking managers and it has been greatly overdone. In the author's experience, top managers are generally reluctant to award perquisites to themselves or to their subordinates for various reasons, including fear that the whole system of company financial control will get out of hand.

Fringe benefits should, and normally do, arise out of the nature of the job. For example, both employees and customers may expect the managing director of a company to have a prestigious car, which is itself a symbol of the company's prosperity. Also, there may be certain types of business functions, conferences and export journeys for which it is in the interests of the company that the managing director should be accompanied by his wife.

Again, if a managing director's pension entitlement is better than the general employee's because it matures to full value after only ten or twenty years of service instead of after forty, this may well be to the advantage of the company. A new managing director may be over forty years old when he is appointed and he may, in some cases, have to be recruited from outside the company. To attract the right man, it will generally be necessary to ensure that his pension matures to full value in a relatively short period.

The general political attack on management in Britain during the 1960s and '70s, through the freezing of top-pay levels, the taxing of fringe benefits and the imposition of very high rates of tax on top-level salaries should not, in the author's view, be regarded too seriously as an attack on the managers themselves. They have been the unfortunate victims of the traditional battle between the organised forces of capital and labour.

To appreciate the significance of this, we need to distinguish between two types of rich people—those who are rich in capital and those who are rich in income. During the years immediately after World War II, nearly all of the Western industrial democracies experimented with penal tax rates on high earned incomes, some of these rates reaching well over 90 per cent. Gradually, however, the more observant governments which were not hidebound by political theory realised that everyone suffered from these high tax rates, not just the unfortunate people called upon to pay them. The work incentive of people in positions of high responsibility, who were rich in income, was seriously impaired, while the people whom these high tax rates were mainly intended to catch, who were rich in capital, were free to escape by moving their official place of residence to a low-tax country. In the process, they usually managed to take some of their capital with them.

Thus, the high-tax country was deprived of both work motivation and availability of industrial capital. Taxation proved to be a blunt and ineffective instrument for redistributing income and wealth. Its popularity as a weapon of social reform declined when people began to see that it operated with particular viciousness against the hard-working resident native of moderate means. Not only could the rich native go abroad, but the rich foreigner could enter the country, buy a mansion and stay for months at a time, without ever becoming a permanent resident and attracting any direct tax payments.

In the late 1960s, there began a trend in major industrial countries, including France, Germany and the United States, towards reducing high tax rates. The milestone in this trend was the American Tax Reform Act of 1969 which progressively brought the top federal earned income tax rate down to 50 per cent . Once a trend of this nature has been followed by a majority of the large Western industrial nations—as it has been—it is difficult for the other industrial nations of the world not to follow as their disadvantageous position for attracting and retaining new enterprise becomes more and more obvious.

16

If the Business is Successful . . .

COULD YOU PASS THROUGH THE EYE OF A NEEDLE?

When Jesus of Nazareth said that it was more difficult for a rich man to enter heaven than for a camel to pass through the eye of a needle, he was apparently referring to a small gate in the wall of Jerusalem, called 'the eye of a needle'. So, his condemnation of riches was not as harsh as at first it sounds. Nevertheless, a managing director must square himself to the fact that if he does a really good job and makes a great success of his business, he may as a reward become rich, and yet at the same time he may be stigmatised by some sections of society for his riches.

How wealthy must a man be to be called rich? Surely not through having a pre-tax income which is five to ten times that of the lowest paid employee? As we saw in Chapter 13, income differentials are well accepted by the great majority of people. More likely, riches become unacceptable when large amounts of capital are accumulated in single hands while at the same time the vast majority of the population are excluded from this process of capital accumulation. In this case, we are not discussing differentials of five to ten times the bottom level, but capital wealth of more than a thousand times the average assets of ordinary people.

We saw in Chapter 11 how, when a business firm's market escalates, capital wealth can be built up very rapidly in the business on a tax-allowable basis. We discussed in Chapter 15

171

the fact that taxation has proved to be a blunt and ineffective instrument for spreading capital wealth. So, the problem for the successful businessman of how to get through the eye of a needle—how to square his actions with his sense of social justice—is likely to be one of how to spread the ownership of his business on a gradual year by year basis so that as and when it grows and accumulates capital, those employees who stay with him and help him to build a substantial business acquire a capital stake in it alongside his own.

One of the saddest sights in modern industry is that of the successful individualist entrepreneur who has never created a true spirit of teamwork or partnership among his employees. He remains an autocrat and sole owner to the end; he then bequeaths much of his wealth to charity. One can hardly object to the charitable gifts as such, but what a commentary they are on the nature of his industrial leadership that he should ignore the very people who helped him to create his wealth!

In the author's experience, the most effective means of sharing with employees the capital growth which occurs in a successful firm is deferred profit-sharing. This is now being put into practice in an increasing number of British firms and there are over 200,000 firms with schemes of this sort in the United States. The system was mentioned briefly in the last chapter, and is now described more fully:

1 A part of the profits, usually around 5 per cent, is set aside to buy shares for employees. These are generally new issue shares, although in some cases they may be shares purchased from an existing holder.
2 The company obtains corporation tax relief on the money set aside.
3 The employee's tax liability on the shares set aside for him and held on his behalf by trustees is deferred until he obtains 'indefeasible right' to the shares. This is usually after three or five years. If he left the firm voluntarily

during this period, he could lose his right to some or all of the shares. If he ceased to be employed for compassionate reasons, such as retirement, incapacity or redundancy, or if he died, he or his estate would retain the shares. Thus the deferral period, in the case of employees who voluntarily stay with the firm, is really a testing time for the 'seedcorn' planted on their behalf. It remains to be seen whether or not their efforts—and good fortune—will result in a plentiful industrial harvest.

4 In the United States, France and Germany, there are tax reliefs for employees who have shares held in schemes of this sort which are then released to them. At the time of writing, similar reliefs are being considered in Britain.

5 Though schemes of this sort would appear to apply mainly in large public companies whose shares have a Stock Exchange listing and a ready market, they can, and are, also run in large private companies in Britain, the United States, France, Germany and other countries. In France they also operate in the nationalised industries. In the case of both large, private-company schemes and nationalised-industry schemes, an internal, regulated share market is established so that employees may, in due course, sell shares back to the trustees of the scheme and thus realise ready-money. The shares sold back are reallotted in the next annual profit-sharing distribution.

In smaller companies a scheme of this sort may involve the issue of redeemable convertible loan stock, partly or wholly instead of shares. The same may sometimes apply in the overseas subsidiaries of multi–national groups.

More details of such schemes are given in Appendix II. In the author's experience, people who already own industrial shares are not usually opposed to employee share schemes. They accept the need for sharing the capital accumulation process if ownership is to be enjoyed by many people and not stigmatised as the privilege of a few.

Objections to share schemes come mainly from people who have been well schooled in economic doctrines which were developed before employee shareholding was considered important. The main objections voiced against such schemes, and the author's comments on them, are as follows:

1 There are those who have been brought up to believe that capital comes from personal saving and that therefore if workers want to own shares they should save up and buy them. As we saw in Chapter 11, this view is no longer tenable. Only 1.1 per cent of capital accumulation over a ten-year period in Britain was found to be through personal saving. All the rest was accumulated by businesses and governments and through pension funds, insurance companies and other institutions, including churches and trade unions.

2 There are those who think of investment purely in stock-market terms and who therefore expect that anyone entitled to a profit-sharing bonus should be free to use it to buy whatever shares he likes, without any obligation to purchase shares in the company employing him.

Every managing director knows, however, that industrial investment is different from stock-market investment. If a company decides to build a new factory and to finance it by reinvesting some of its profits, and if at the same time some of these profits are 'capitalised' by the issue of shares to employees, it is not possible for any of the company's shareholders, be they employees or otherwise, to opt out of the investment decision. Imagine somebody approaching the managing director and saying: 'I do not agree with your idea of a new factory; I want to invest elsewhere, so you can leave off part of the roof and give me money instead'!

In the corporate world, the typical pay-back period for new investment calculations is seven years, so any industrial employee who has shares allocated to him, representing part of the reinvested profits, must expect to wait several years before he can benefit from them. Some employees will not want to sell their shares when they are released, so a compulsory holding period can usually be much shorter than the average pay-back period. A better alternative to a compulsory holding period is a tax rate which reduces with the length of time that the shares are held, thus encouraging employees to hold on and pay a lower rate of tax. This is discussed more fully in Appendix II.

3 There are those who say that the use of part of the profits of a business to subscribe for shares for employees means diluting the equity of the existing shareholders and making the company a bad investment for outsiders, including the employee pension funds. It must be admitted that if too great a percentage of profits is used in this way, the equity is diluted. However, the mathematical work of Thunen in the last century, set out in Appendix II, suggests that a modest level of deferred profit-sharing actually improves the rewards of both capital and labour. This seems to be borne out by the only study made of the performance of deferred profit-sharing companies in comparison with companies which had no such schemes. This research was done in the United States by B. L. Metzger and J. A. Colletti, and their results are presented in Appendix II. It would therefore appear that diluting the equity does not arise from the mere act of using profits to buy shares for employees, but from doing this to excess—beyond what is known as the Thunen equilibrium point.

Having examined the three principal objections to deferred profit-sharing and commented on them, we now turn to the five major reasons why this is an important aspect of motivating and rewarding employees.

1 The proportion of the population owning shares and therefore having direct experience of the role of capital in

industry is small in most countries. In Britain it is particularly low, for only 3.8 per cent of people of working age or above own any industrial shares (see p 129). Business enterprise cannot expect to function effectively when the great majority of people lack an important type of experience which could make them feel fully part of the industrial system.

2 As we saw in Chapter 10, a considerable amount of the fixed industrial investment made by industry is financed by government subsidies and tax allowances of various kinds. It is surely wrong that the existing body of shareholders, whoever they are, should be the sole direct beneficiaries from this use of taxpayers' money. The nearest and most obvious group with whom they could be asked to share their good fortune is the employees.

3 In Chapter 12 we discussed the problem of how to motivate a labour force which has an on-site monopoly. This discussion was carried further in Chapters 13 and 14 where we developed systems of earnings progression and value added pay. A monopoly labour force needs systems of this sort to turn it from what could be a potentially sullen and destructive group, an alternative centre of authority in the business, into a co-operative and united team striving for the same goals as the top management of the business and rewarded in the same general manner—with the prospect of both higher cash income and capital accumulation if the firm is successful.

4 In Chapter 14 we discussed a value added pay system and two crucial questions: how to determine the normal ratio of value added to employee costs and the use of a Bonus Grid to relate employee bonus to both value added profitability. When a managing director is reaching his decisions on these issues, ready for explanation and discussion with employee representatives, he inevitably finds that there is an area of possible dispute, where employees could say that their cash earnings should be greater; the company's

management could reply that if the employees take more in cash, they will be eating some of the seedcorn, and add that there would not be enough cash left for investment and, as a consequence, the future harvest would be poor for everyone.

This argument over seedcorn is central to the issue of what should be labour's total share. As there is an area where nobody can be certain what is the right point of division, the best solution to this argument, in the author's experience, is to ask the question: 'Why not share the ownership of the seedcorn?'. This means, in effect, that employees can have the benefit of this area of uncertainty if they take their earnings in seedcorn and not in cash.

5 We discussed in Chapter 9 the modern problem of trying to maintain full employment without inflation and it was indicated that more would be said about this in Chapter 16. It is the author's belief that a significant factor in preventing the achievement of full employment without causing inflation is the extent of alienation of the labour force from the industrial system. High profits are needed if firms are to achieve adequate investment and create further employment opportunities, and yet high profits are frowned upon by a labour movement whose members own hardly any of the shares to which those profits are attributable. From the general theory of employment developed in the 1930s by John Maynard Keynes, we have learnt that a high level of unemployment may be partly due to the fact that the profitability of industry, measured in terms of its ability to pay dividends, is below the rate of interest. When this occurs, the labour movement's intolerance of high profits is a factor in causing unemployment and hence it leads to inflationary spending by government in a vain attempt to cure the unemployment. The attempt is vain because industry has little incentive to invest and thereby create more jobs when the earnings yield on its current investments is below the rate of interest payable on borrowed money.

177

Higher profits could, in the author's view, be more easily tolerated by the labour movement if they were manifestly sharing in those profits. So, again we come back to the role of deferred profit-sharing in enabling employees to participate in the profits and build up a shareholding without taking out of the business the cash needed for investment. Employee share-ownership schemes in the larger firms would therefore appear to be a possible aid to the maintenance of a full-employment policy without inflation.

17

Team Motivation

This book cannot tell the reader the secret he most wants to know—how to find the winning product or service which will escalate wildly and make him a fortune, more or less in the manner described in Chapter 11. Like every other member of business management, he must keep on at the competitive hunt for the right combination of product features which meet a need at the right quality and price, in the right place and time. He can always hope that he will be lucky but he must know that he may never be.

The most that this book can do is to provide the reader with a set of management practices which aid the running of a business and which, at the same time, add up to a comprehensive philosophy of modern enterprise. Why is it necessary to have a management philosophy? Surely one can continue with the habits of the 1950s and '60s, developing techniques and practices to cope with particular circumstances, without caring a jot for overall principles?

To continue in this way is a recipe for disaster. The business world has, for nearly a century, been on the defensive—in some countries on the run—from the organised forces of centralism. An extraordinary situation has developed in which a tiny handful of people who are fervent believers in certain political philosophies have been able to hold industry to ransom, use the power of the State to take over business firms

179

and put independent enterprise into shackles which discourage and inhibit its major role of serving customers effectively and efficiently.

It is the author's conviction that a small minority of people have been able to do this because business has not had, for well over 100 years, an adequate philosophy to describe the standards of conduct of the typical enterprise which is both commercially successful and also socially acceptable in its behaviour towards those who work in the business. There are thousands of firms which reach high standards in these respects. What has been needed is an integrated philosophy, bringing together the key points of accepted practice.

In the two centuries since the time of Adam Smith, the reigning philosophy of independent business enterprise has been arch individualism, as portrayed in the typical story of the all-successful, all-powerful, self-made multi–millionaire who has risen from rags to riches within a period of ten to twenty years. Examples of this type are included in Appendix I. However, the rags to riches story is relatively rare and it leaves out of account the role of thousands of managing directors who are also successful but less single-minded—who are interested in running a team enterprise where people actually like to work.

The need for a philosophy of team enterprise would be strong even if business had not been on the defensive. A coherent set of beliefs is an aid to building both confidence and purpose. A large and important leadership group, such as managing directors, cannot hope to be both commercially successful and socially acceptable unless a major part of their beliefs are work-a-day principles which set high standards of human behaviour.

From where can an appropriate set of principles be derived? In the author's view, they must come from a correct analysis of the political situation in which industry is placed. This is widely viewed, particularly in Britain, as a battle between centralism and individualism, between those who want power centralised in the State and those who want power dispersed among individuals.

The author's analysis is somewhat different, as will have become apparent from the earlier chapters of this book. He believes that the battle is between the forces of centralism and the forces of decentralisation, and that the real focus of decentralisation should not be on the individual alone, but on the individual and his place in the enterprise. The main champion of individual freedom must be an organisation, not a person, though it will usually be headed by a person—the managing director.

No MD can hope to escape from politics. He is right at the centre of the battle over the dispersal of power. Unless this battle is won, there is little prospect for personal freedom. Individuals cannot hope to win without the enterprise. Most people cannot stand on their own, but need to be part of a working team. It is therefore the business leader's unavoidable task to integrate the needs of the individual with those of the working team.

Managing directors are personally involved in a problem which appears to be rapidly approaching the centre of the human stage. Look at these challenging words of Dr Franley Lesse from the USA at the International Congress of Psychiatrists, Honolulu, August 1977:

If today's rugged individualists, self-made-men and local boys made good, took a time-machine trip to the year 2000, they would probably be given immediate psychiatric attention. Within two generations the individual ego will be superseded in importance by the group ego. Individualists will be looked upon as odd and reactionary, and personal success will be defined as being part of a successfully functioning group.

When the theory of enterprise was developed, the business firm was generally identified with a person, a manufacturer

181

or trader who usually had very few staff but who employed many 'hands' to do the physical work, as the following passage from Adam Smith's *Wealth of Nations* reveals:

> In every improved society, the farmer is generally nothing but a farmer; the manufacturer nothing but a manufacturer. The labour, too, which is necessary to produce any one complete manufacture is almost always divided among a great number of hands.

Today, however, this would be widely regarded as a nonsense description of the real situation in a business of any significant size. There are relatively few 'hands'. As we have already seen, half the population has white-collar jobs. Although the other half is officially classed as blue collar, or manual, a large number of these jobs involve skills and responsibilities that entail the sophisticated co-ordination of mental and manual activities. In short, the 'blues' are partly 'white' and many of them have acquired white-collar attitudes towards pay differentials, incentives and personal ownership.

What have the white-collar workers learnt from the 'blues'? Mainly, that they are a team who should not be afraid of losing their individualism if they take group action. Indeed, they need to stand together over matters of pay so that they cannot be picked off as individuals.

A strong characteristic of all teams is that they abhor the victimisation of individuals, so they tend to make rules which protect the individual as a member of the group. One of the most recent examples in Britain of group rule-making is the establishment of a committee of chairmen of nationalised industries. Without such a committee, chairmen could be individually dealt with by government ministers and left powerless to react effectively against unfair squeezing of their personal living-standards or arbitrary cuts in the capital expenditure programmes of their industries.

In the 200 years since Adam Smith, the growth of corporate

pay and career structures has destroyed much of his theory of wages. He described a situation in which labourers were paid the going market rate for their hire and they could always expect to be paid this. If the market rate went up, anyone who did not receive a rise could cease working and wait in the market to be re-engaged at the new rate of pay.

Today, however, most of us work in organisations where we stay for many years, if not for our full working lives. Even those who change jobs have to give, or be given, notice of termination. The corporate wage and salary structure, as discussed in Chapter 13, bears little relation to a free market in labourers. None of us knows whether, if we resigned our jobs, we would obtain another job in a matter of months or years, and if we were lucky in doing so, whether the pay for the job would be more or less than we had recently been earning. Older people would strongly suspect that they might earn less in their next job, even if they had been financially well-treated and had been very valuable to their previous employer.

So the modern managing director has to lead a team which is not for the most part on a hire-and-fire basis, which does not have its pay levels completely determined in the labour market and which insists on having a pay and career structure. It insists on behaving as a group even when it is not formally organised in a trade union. The group or team ethic would require at least a staff association, even if trade unions had never been invented.

The nature of the team ethic and its relationship to the individualist ethic is seen when we examine the effect of a company's pay structure on employees' willingness to work. It was indicated in Chapter 13 that we must distinguish carefully between the level of pay which is necessary to recruit a person into a job and the type of pay structure which may be necessary to motivate him, both as an individual and as a team member, once he is in the job. The more successful the pay structure is at motivating employees, the more prosperous the firm is likely to be and the less risk of the company's pay levels slipping below the recruitment levels. This may happen occasionally when a job is wrongly valued, but it will be a rarity and is easily dealt with.

By contrast, if a firm is unsuccessful with its pay structure as a motivator, it is likely to be less successful as a commercial enterprise, and so its pay levels are in greater danger of slipping below the basic recruitment levels. Merely to raise pay across the board in these circumstances is an unsatisfactory answer. It may temporarily cure the recruitment problem until pay levels elsewhere are also raised, but it does nothing for the motivation to work, either for the individual career-seeker or for his sense of belonging to a working team which is rewarded as a team for its achievements.

A managing director must aim to build a basic team which stays together and has a rate of staff turnover which is no more than adequate to cope with the problems of individual, personal dissatisfaction—the unavoidable square peg in the round hole. Much of the effectiveness of a working team lies in the fact that members know each other, that they each hold a part of the total know-how and they are therefore able to to contribute effectively to each other's tasks. A high rate of employee turnover is a serious economic loss.

So the managing director's interest in satisfying the needs of both the individualist ethic and the team ethic is possibly as great as that of team members and of their representative organisations, the unions. But the approach is likely to be different. The MD's attitude to the team must be: 'I want you as a team, you and only you, in sickness and in health, till retirement do us part. Individual members may leave the team and I will occasionally dismiss one. I will also select the new recruits, but subject to this I accept the team for what it is— warts and all. In witness to this, I am prepared to design incentives which satisfy both individual and group needs.'

This attitude of acceptance of the working team for what it is—an on-site monopoly labour force—is widespread among the more successful family businesses. It is summed up in the words of a director of one of the largest and most successful private companies in England: 'We believe that these ideas of team sharing are particularly important when employees become committed to the company—for life—when we know and they know that they are not going to move again.'

Failing this attitude of acceptance by the managing director, the trade union attitude is likely to be: 'Here is an employer who concentrates solely on the individualist ethic. He picks off our people one at a time, provides incentives and special rewards for certain key people whom he fears might leave and pays the remainder as sparingly as possible. He is particularly tight with the older folk who could not easily get another job if they did leave. So we will set up an alternative centre of authority in his firm and teach him a lesson or two about the team ethic.'

The key to recognition of both the individualist ethic and the team ethic lies in the pay structure, not only because pay is important but also because it epitomises a managing director's attitude to most other aspects of human relations. His pay structure should reflect the success of the firm and it should be designed to encourage employees to stay with the firm. At the same time, it should not put any major obstacles in the way of anyone who feels that he must leave. There are likely to be four parts to any well designed pay structure. It should contain:

1 A system of individual earnings progression, to satisfy personal career needs.
2 A system of group earnings progression, to satisfy team desire that they should all change in pay together, in accord with changing prices and productivity.
3 Individual participation in capital growth, particularly in the larger firms, so that an employee's loyalty to the team during a successful period of enterprise is rewarded with capital, more or less in line with the growth in shareholders' capital.

185

4 Group provision for the future, typically via a pension scheme and life insurance, so that the team is seen to provide its members with some security.

Although this total pay package looks expensive, in fact it need not necessarily involve any additional cost at the moment of introduction. A key point about it is that it should be structured to involve additional cost only when this is earned by the achievements of the individual employees and of the team.

In shaping his total pay structure, the managing director must be prepared to accept that some of it cannot be fully effective without government legislation. Nevertheless, this should not deter him from setting it up and from pressing for the right government measures. Of particular relevance is the need for some tax relief for accumulated employee share capital. In conditions where the vast majority of the population has no experience of acquiring and holding share capital, there is clearly room for experimenting with a modest concession which encourages this. Indeed, the successful establishment of a means of maintaining a wide spread of industrial ownership throughout the community would seem to be almost as essential to the permanent establishment of democracy as is the right to vote.

Adam Smith's analysis of events external to the firm—of the importance of competition, the role of the market in determining prices and costs, and the distribution of resources—is still almost entirely valid. What he could not have foreseen was the tremendous developments which would take place in the requirements for teamwork within the business enterprise. The biggest surprise for Smith, if he were to return today, might be to find that good teamwork is not the death-knell of individualism, but rather its flowering. There are few individuals who can be complete except in the setting of a team.

No theory of enterprise can now be adequate if it confines itself to how the market operates. It must also take into account how the managing director operates—the type of team organisation which he runs. Unless this kind of approach is accepted, independent enterprise cannot be expected to stand up to the onslaughts of the centralists. A modern enterprise must not only strive to remain independent and competitive in its dealing with customers, it must also strive to be socially just in its dealings with employees. The team ethic is the key to the survival of the individualist ethic. Adam Smith's competitive economic system has, by and large, given to firms the rewards they deserve, but this is not the same thing as giving to employees the rewards they deserve, both as individuals and as team members.

While acting as champion of independent enterprise, the managing director need not, and indeed should not, turn his back on State enterprise. He will almost certainly want the unrelenting growth of State enterprise to be brought to a halt, but he will recognise that there are occasions when the State's financial power and even its monopoly power may be necessary for the establishment and continuing survival of a particular type of industry. Moreover, he will recognise that State enterprise must be tailored to the needs of a basically competitive system.

Hopefully, he will want to encourage an extension of the French experiment in creating employee share schemes within State enterprises, such as Renault. When President de Gaulle set up these schemes, he also expressed a hope that, in due time, we would see the union of all Europe 'from the Atlantic to the Urals'. Clearly de Gaulle had a vision that if the West could set an example in establishing the same systems within State industry as in private, the day might come when at least one East European country would take note and act. When that happened, we could begin the long process of reconciliation of East and West, with the prospect of privately owned and State owned industry working side by side, united by the fact that they both had employee shareholders and both operated within a market economy extending across Europe.

187

Modern industry's managing directors are unavoidably key figures in any plan for preserving world peace by reconciling East and West. This does not mean that they must play an active role in party politics. They have their own unique part to play in evolving a union between the individualist ethic and the team ethic, establishing the principles on which this union can be based and then putting them into practice. This is an inspiring cause with which to light up the world. It is doubly inspiring because it can appeal to both the mind and the purse.

Appendix I

Casebook of Business Achievement

The following examples of business achievement taken from the Press illustrate both the rapid growth of successful businesses and the fast rate of capital accumulation sometimes achieved.

Mr Ray Turner, 43-year-old chairman of the Ray Turner Group, has had his life insured by the company for £2.25m to cover death duties on his large personal shareholding should he die suddenly.

For technical reasons Mr Turner had to reduce his controlling stake of 50.9 per cent to 49.9 per cent by selling 27,000 shares on Monday.

He started the group—which has interests in employment agencies, games, school equipment and stationery—from scratch in 1963 and it has a current market value of about £6m.

The Financial Times, 13 December 1972

Mr and Mrs Gubay moved to the Isle of Man early in 1972 and it is therefore felt that some of the near £11.5m they have realized may not be subject to capital gains tax.

In all, with the proceeds of the offer for sale when Kwik Save went public in November 1970, and some other small share sales, Mr Gubay has realised between £13m and £14m in the last two years.

Kwik Save has its origins in a confectionery business set up by Mr Gubay in the early 1950s. In 1962, he went into US-style drive-in supermarkets, but in 1965 made a radical change of direction into a highly successful method of discount supermarkets under the Kwik Save name.

This set the stage for a rapid profit rise from £19,000 in the year to August 1965 to £1.6m in 1971–72.

The Financial Times, 2 January 1973

Francis Holmes is, he claims, the first self-made millionaire to emerge from the North Sea oil fields. His story, so far, is a little classic of its kind: six years ago, at the age of 23, he borrowed £1,000 from his mother and bought a Yarmouth electrical contracting concern 'running around houses and wiring lights'. Then, during the 1968 house building slump he switched to industrial work and a year later got his first contract on a North Sea oil rig. From then on it was a case of growing up with the oil fields to the point when yesterday his EAE Group was big enough to command a £900,000 price tag from the Bonochord electrical and electronic group . . .

Holmes becomes a millionaire through his stake, plus property investments, including a night club in the Canary Islands, he has made on the security of the oil business.

The Financial Times, 22 March 1973

Rumours are buzzing in the rag trade that 36 year old Mr Irvine Sellar, the one-time market trader who has built up the Mates women's and men's fashionwear group, is about to clinch his biggest deal yet.

I hear that negotiations are almost complete for Mates to take over another shop group in the same line of business at a cost of around £2 million.

This former RAF national serviceman, who started selling clothing at a stall in Hitchin market, is already a member of the exclusive millionaires' club, having built Mates into a multi-million pound group.

Mr Sellar borrowed a few hundred pounds in 1957 to get the stall at Hitchin going. Soon he was operating at most of the well-known street markets in the London area.

Evening News, 7 May 1973

17 years ago Ralph Weston bought his second shop.

They've been busy years for Ralph Weston. Since 1956 he has systematically acquired existing chemists chains, opened new shops, modernised layouts and closed less profitable outlets. Today he has a chemist network second only to Boots: 200 shops and more to come.

But Westons is more than just shops. It is one of Britain's major pharmaceutical wholesalers, with a turnover around £25 million, serving 6,000 chemists. During last year alone, this side of the business was virtually trebled and this expansion will continue.

At the same time, Westons saw the value to themselves and their customers of producing their own brands. So today you can find a range of Weston products, including toothpaste, tissues, shampoos and hairsprays.

Add to this some highly successful subsidiaries, like Hedges, the snuff manufacturers, and Permaflex who make butane gas refills and you have the basis for Weston's consistent record of increased earnings.

The Financial Times, 1 June 1973

At 29, Malcolm Webster and John Robinson are retiring— each worth around £600,000 before capital gains tax. Not bad for eight years' work, don't you think?

They are the first of the jean revolution's youthful entrepreneurs to take the money and run. Well, not run, exactly, more saunter away whistling a happy tune. They have just sold their leisure wear company called Steepleglade to Siebe Gorman Holdings for £1.1m down plus another £150,000 if profits this year do as expected and hit £750,000. It makes you sick.

Their story started in 1969 when they were near-penniless agricultural students who decided that it was going to be very difficult making money farming. So they started up making clothes in Putney, West London.

Just like that? Apparently. The timing was lucky, but they must have had flair. Their first success was in blue cotton from Morocco (remember that?), then came Loon Pants in wide, white cotton drill, followed by embroidered denim and the two-button graded vest. The past three years have been predominantly jeans, with the two young entrepreneurs promoting their Inega label with unbelievable success.

Now their company has a factory at Hirwaun in Gwent, £650,000 in assets, a turnover approaching £4.5m—and is the proud new possession of Siebe Gorman. Barry Stephens, the Welsh-American managing director of the public holding company, thinks he has a bargain. Steepleglade, he says, is the most promising leisure operation in Western Europe today. It's not a cute business, it's wholesome. This is where the money is, he says.

It isn't, of course. I know where it is. In Webster and Robinson's pockets.

The Sunday Times, 20 March 1977

Good industrial relations usually result from years of painstaking endeavour. Sometimes there may be a watershed beyond which relations improve dramatically, but to maintain this improvement requires sustained effort from both sides.

Fluidrive Engineering Company of Isleworth and Bracknell provide an example of this process, which makes fluid couplings. In 1973 it endured a three months' work to rule which sent pre-tax profits down from £489,000 to £289,000.

In October that year a new managing director, Richard Miles was appointed, and under his guidance a more participative approach to relations with the shopfloor workers has developed. Since then turnover has doubled and pre-tax profits have risen from £289,000 to £787,000.

It would be simplistic to relate these improved figures in too direct a fashion to a changed industrial relations environment, but at least it can be said that the move from a year in which there was a three months' work to rule to a period of three-and-a-half years in which the loss of productive time through disputes has been negligible must have contributed greatly to the improved profits.

The Times, 15 August 1977

To-day Cavenham shareholders vote on the scheme whereby Generale Occidentale stands to increase its equity interest in the company from 75 to 100 per cent. The proposals were, apparently, dreamed up by Sir James Goldsmith's financial advisers while the maestro was away on holiday. Last year, the fact that a deal between the two increased GO's holding from 39 to just over 50 per cent, was similarly presented as a lucky chance: it was, a Goldsmith aide claimed at the time, a pure coincidence that the transaction gave GO a majority of the votes.

Yet the remarkable fact remains that Cavenham—a company which in the past decade has built its gross assets up from £12m to over £500m—has throughout its development remained firmly within the control of GO and its main shareholder, Sir James Goldsmith. A major multi–national food company has been established, mainly by a series of acquisitions, without diluting the equity interest of the entrepreneur responsible for it all. Now it seems likely that the final act is about to take place, with the base of the pyramid being absorbed by its own apex.

The Financial Times, 12 September 1977

It is ironic that even as knives are being sharpened for major surgery on British Rail's heavily loss-making parcels business, a small private company should be heading for yet another record year under its wing.

What City Link offers is very simple. It provides a nation-wide parcels collection and delivery service for customers who are prepared to pay for the unrivalled speed and reliability of British Rail's Red Star express parcels service, which operates only from station to station. Unlike Rail Express Parcels ordinary services, Red Star is both profitable and, because goods are booked on specific passenger trains, tightly controlled . . .

The idea of adding a fast and flexible collect and delivery arm to the Red Star backbone came initially from a mini-cab operator, who formed City Link in 1969. Two years later, having mainly limited itself to business in the London area, the company had debts of £10,000 and was up for sale.

Mr Bob Thomas, then 32, with wide experience of the air freight business, bought 75 per cent of the company for £75. Within a year, the company was free of its inherited debts and on a development path which is expected this year to produce profits of £150,000 on a turnover of about £1m.

The Financial Times, 20 September 1977

Aviation has always produced a rich harvest of pioneers, on both the aircraft manufacturing and the airline operational sides of the industry. In recent years, new opportunities have emerged in the rapidly expanding field of air cargo world-wide, and as a result a new generation of innovators is appearing, some of whom have already made a significant impact.

One of these is Alan Stocks, the founder and chairman of what is now Britain's biggest all-freight aviation operation, IAS Cargo Airlines, the trading title for International Aviation Services (UK).

Now aged 47, Stocks founded IAS in 1966, initially to supply a wide range of support services in the aviation industry, from management consultancy to brokerage. Later, the company moved into the aircraft operating field, and in 1970–71, with only one Britannia turbo-prop freighter, it earned a pre-tax profit of £15,000 on a turnover of £215,000. By 1976–77, with a partially-leased fleet of three DC-8 and three Boeing 707 jets, one Britannia, one CL-44 and a Super Hercules, it earned a pre-tax profit of £510,000 on a turnover of £23m.

The Financial Times, 20 September 1977

Appendix II

Optimum Reward for the Company and its Employees

It was claimed in Chapter 14 that through the issue of shares to employees on a limited scale not exceeding the Thunen equilibrium point, companies could be more successful and there would be no dilution of the equity. Both shareholders and employees gained and evidence is given here in favour of this claim. It is, however, placed in its context. First, the basic method of issuing shares to employees, through a profit-linked share plan, is described. Secondly, the principles behind this method are presented, together with the evidence of the Metzger study, the Thunen mathematics and the author's own study of capital formation over a ten-year period in Britain. Lastly, a number of extracts are presented from documents which illustrate the development of a logical approach to tax treatment for employee share schemes.

Profit-linked Share Plans for Employees
The following is a general description of how profit-linked share plans work, though each one must be tailored to the specific needs of the company.

1 A part of the annual profits is set aside and used via trustees to buy new issue shares, or in some cases shares already issued, which are allocated to specific employees.

2 The profits set aside are allowable for corporation tax as a cost to the company.

3 The shares are held in trust for a period, usually five years.
4 At the end of the deferral period, the employee obtains 'indefeasible right'. He can pay tax, at whatever rate is applicable, on a 'receipts' basis, which means he pays only on the value received. If, therefore, the shares have gone down in value, tax is paid only on the reduced value.
5 If the employee leaves the company before the end of the five-year period for compassionate reasons such as retirement, redundancy or ill-health, or if he dies, he obtains indefeasible right to all the shares allocated to him.
6 If the employee leaves the company before the end of the five-year period for other reasons, such as seeking alternative employment, he receives indefeasible right only to those shares which have 'vested' in him. It is usual to have 'graduated vesting'. For example, if full vesting occurs after five years, a person leaving after three years obtains indefeasible right to three-fifths of the shares allocated to him three years ago, and to two-fifths of the shares allocated two years ago, and so on.
7 Shares which do not vest are reallocated by the trustees among the employees who remain. Experience shows that this reallocation is an important factor in employee asset formation. Long-service employees of a successful company can eventually own a holding which is very significant to them, although it may be a very small fraction of the company's total shareholding.

Schemes of the above kind were first developed in Britain by the author for Habitat, Bulmer, House of Fraser, and other companies in the period 1975–8. At the time of this book going to press, such schemes, known as Method III in a government consultative document, are the subject of legislation in the 1978 Finance Bill, so that the amount set aside to buy shares for an employee earns tax relief if he holds the shares for five years or more.

Basic Principles of Employee Share Ownership
Several important points of basic principles are discussed in this section and the available evidence is presented, in support of the answers.

Does it pay to have employee shareholders?
Companies which have employee share schemes are on the whole more productive and more profitable than those which do not. This has been shown in a major American study by B. L. Metzger and J. A. Colletti, in which two samples of companies were compared. They were of similar types and sizes except that sample A were all companies in which employee shareholding was significant and sample B were all companies in which there were no employee shareholders.

The study was conducted over an eighteen-year period, 1952–69, during which time the companies in both samples grew in earnings per share, market price and other accepted measures of performance. But the companies in sample A grew faster. The following table shows the superior growth of the sample A companies over the sample B companies. This reveals that at the end of the eighteen-year period, the shareholders in companies where the employees also were shareholders found that their shares had grown nearly twice as fast in market price as the shares of the companies in which the employees had no stake.

One can try to discount this study by saying that perhaps the sample A companies were better managed than the sample B companies. Perhaps they were, but over an eighteen-year period the management of a business changes quite considerably. How many boards of directors are the same after eighteen years?

The figures of this American survey fall into line with those of a survey conducted by the Confederation of British Industry, and published in April 1976. This showed that 86 per cent of British employees thought that industry would be more productive if employees had a stake in its profits.

COMPARATIVE GROWTH OF COMPANIES WITH AND
WITHOUT EMPLOYEE SHAREHOLDERS (OVER THE
EIGHTEEN-YEAR PERIOD 1952–69)

	Sample A Companies with Employee Shareholders (1952=100)	Sample B Companies without Employee Shareholders (1952=100)
Index of market price per share (1969)	782.1	397.6
Index of earnings per share (1969)	410.5	218.8
Index of balance sheet net worth per share (1969)	376.1	256.7
Index of sales revenue (1969)	358.4	266.0

Why is it necessary even to consider having employee shareholders?

A well managed company which treats its employees fairly may postpone indefinitely the question of creating employee shareholders. If every company does this, however, the number of people in the community with experience of shareholding is likely to remain very low. This is virtually what has happened in Britain, with the result that there is widespread misunderstanding of the role of capital in industry and there is a lower level of productivity than in the United States of America or Germany.

Only 3.8 per cent of the adults entitled to vote at a general election in Britain directly own shares in British Industry. This figure comes from a survey of personal savings and wealth in Great Britain conducted by Professor E. Victor Morgan and published by *The Financial Times* in 1975. Morgan's figure is lower than the equivalent figure of 4.7 per cent derived from a survey commissioned by the Stock Exchange, London, and published in 1966. Most experts agree that personal shareholding has been declining.

199

The country with by far the most experience of employee shareholding is the United States, where no less than 200,000 companies have voluntarily set up schemes. Most of the growth in number of share schemes has occurred during the last decade and, using the New York Stock Exchange survey conducted in 1975 as a basis, it can now be estimated that 25 per cent of Americans of working age or above have a direct interest in shares.

In France, President de Gaulle applied a similar system to companies with 100 employees or more, and he also applied a modified version of it to nationalised firms such as Renault. The French proportion of shareholders was similar to the British ten years ago, but it is now 9.2 per cent.

In Germany, there is a rather different system for employee capital-building at the place of work and 18 million employees are participators. The initiative for this system came from a trade union leader and there are now 260 agreements between unions and employers relating to employee capital-building. The German system includes money put into special bank accounts but this aspect is hardly relevant to Britain. Nevertheless, the German system has resulted in the proportion of shareholders rising to 7.6 per cent.

Britain is an 'under-developed country' as far as employee shareholding is concerned. There are only about 100 schemes for general employee shareholding and most of these are of a type which leads to only about 10 per cent of employees participating. It is hardly surprising that Britain's proportion of shareholders is only 3.8 per cent.

Should not employees save up to buy shares?
It is unrealistic to expect employees to save money from their take-home pay in order to buy shares. This is not an urgent use of their funds as is, for example, family expenditure. Only just over 1 per cent of the total addition to national capital in Britain each year comes from discretionary saving by private persons. The greatest capital accumulators are companies,

followed by government authorities. This was revealed in a paper prepared by the author for the British North-American Research Association and entitled *The Changing Pattern of Savings and Investment in the United Kingdom,* as already mentioned in Chapter 1. The following table is taken from an article in *The Times,* 26 August 1976, summarising this paper.

BRITISH NATIONAL CAPITAL ACCUMULATION
1965–1974

A Contributions from the Non-personal Sectors of the Economy

		Per Cent
1	Capital accumulation by companies	36.1
2	Capital accumulation by public corporations	8.7
3	Capital accumulation by central government	17.6
4	Capital accumulation by local authorities	5.3
	Total capital accumulation by the non-personal sectors	67.7

B Contributions from the Personal Sectors of the Economy

5	Capital accumulation through pension policies and (estimated) related life assurance	9.7
6	Capital accumulation through home mortgage repayments	7.2
7	Domestic depreciation provisions	5.5
8	Depreciation provisions by the self-employed	3.4
9	Additional (estimated) capital accumulation by the self-employed	4.3
10	Capital accumulation by non-profit bodies	1.1
11	Possible genuine personal saving (ie the remainder of the Blue Book estimate of total personal saving)	1.1
	Total capital accumulation by the personal sectors	32.3
	Total all sectors	100.0

The case for employees being aided by the company in becoming shareholders is summarised in an EEC commission report entitled *Asset Formation Policy* released early in 1976, from which the following English translation extract is taken:

45 A new objective, which is being increasingly adopted in the member states, challenges the traditional view of how profit should be used and distributed. Company profits have in recent years been increasingly reinvested in the business, both to accelerate the depreciation of assets and to finance growth. This has made it possible to cope with the requirements of technological progress and of obsolescence and at the same time maintain a high level of employment.

However, it is being ever more seriously questioned whether the resulting increase in self-financed assets should bring capital appreciation only to the existing shareholders—a situation which leads to the concentration of industrial shareholding—whilst employees of the company receive, apart from their salaries and wages no share in this capital appreciation, though they have contributed to this growth of wealth and made it possible for the company to further its equipment programme. A general objective of industry must therefore be to devise a better way of sharing out the results of productive enterprise amongst all the parties concerned.

Does employee shareholding result in dilution of the equity?
Provided that the reasonable limits (see p 211) are adhered to, employee shareholding should not result in dilution of the equity. As the Metzger study reported on p 199 shows, both shareholders and employees usually gain because companies which have employee shareholders usually perform better than those which do not.

In recognition of the fact that existing equity is not diluted, schemes for employee shareholding in Britain are sometimes referred to as 'participation in capital growth'. The official title for the French programme in this area is *Participation des Salariés aux Fruits de l'Expansion'*. In the United States, the programme has been entitled by the Joint Economic Committee of Congress 'Broadening the Ownership of New Capital'.

Is it not unwise for employees to put all their eggs in one basket?

In a welfare state where virtually all the economic misfortunes that might befall employees are covered by social security benefits, one cannot be overly concerned about the possibility of employees losing money on company shares which have come to them through a share scheme. If the scheme involved saving money out of take-home pay, there would be more cause for concern, but typically today a scheme is likely to involve deferred profit-sharing.

The usual period of deferment, during which time the employee is required to hold the shares allocated to him, is no more than five years. After this time he can, if he wishes, sell his shares and either spend the money or buy other securities.

If he chooses to diversify his holding by buying other securities, then in a working life of forty years, five annual profit-sharing allocations will be invested in shares of the company where he works and the other thirty-five will be spread throughout a range of other investments. Even a senior employee who does not join a share scheme until ten years before retirement will have half his investments diversified by the time he retires and he can steadily diversify the remainder after that. Thus, it cannot be said that share schemes generally result in an employee having 'all his eggs in one basket'.

Why should employees be obliged to take shares when they might prefer cash?

A business owner who decides to bequeath shares to his children does not ask himself: 'Would they prefer cash?' He recognises that someone must take the responsibility for owning the business. If he thinks his children might take an irresponsible attitude and sell their shares too soon, he puts the shares in trust until the children are of a more mature age.

The same principle is used in employee share schemes. If it is considered a good idea that employees should be shareholders, but if at the same time there is a fear that they may sell their shares for instant cash, it is reasonable to impose a required holding period. This is an accepted and time-honoured practice in human history, as these examples show:

1 Whenever a country has instituted land reform in order to break up large landholdings, the peasants who have received allocations of land have been required to hold them for a period.
2 When the western plains of the United States were settled, under the Homestead Acts a settler could obtain 640 acres of free land on condition that he lived on the land, worked it and retained it for a period of years, and did not sell it for instant cash to speculators.
3 In Britain today, when council houses are sold to sitting tenants on favourable terms, there is usually a requirement that they must hold the house for five years.

Can employees really build up a shareholding which is significant enough to influence their attitude to enterprise?

Experience of launching company schemes for employee shareholding shows that if a scheme is well launched, with briefing meetings for employees and the issue of an explanatory booklet, even the launching of the scheme can have an important effect on attitudes. An employee who goes home and tells his family that he is going to be a shareholder in the business has, in some sense, taken on a new image in their eyes.

When Crawford Greenewalt was president of Du Pont in the 1950s, he developed the concept of 'the owner's eye' as applied to industry. He found that the typical senior employee of a company looked upon it as his own business when he had acquired a shareholding which was significant to him, in relation to his other assets and income, even if this was a very small shareholding in relation to the total number of issued shares.

Both managers and long-service employees of all grades do build up shareholdings through an employee share scheme which causes them to feel that they own the company. A typical scheme favours accumulation of shares by the long-service employee.

Should all employees participate in a share scheme or only selected groups?
For most favourable tax treatment in Britain, the Inland Revenue requires that 'all or most' employees participate, and 'most' is interpreted strictly as no less than a bare majority. In some companies with a high turnover of employees, this can mean all employees with just over one year's service. In a more stable enterprise, the bare majority will be achieved by including only employees with four or five years' service.

General experience with share schemes is that it is best to include as many employees as possible, subject to a minimum period of service such as one year. This has two purposes:

1 It ensures that all those who participate in the scheme have been working with the company for sufficient time to be able to contribute to its profitability.
2 It keeps out of the administration of the scheme the short-term employees.

After an employee has begun to participate in a share scheme, there is usually a further qualifying period of a few years before he becomes fully entitled to any shares allocated to his name. In other words, full entitlement involves the completion of further service. This is an important reason for keeping to a minimum the initial period of service required before an employee participates in a scheme.

Does a share scheme mean that the employees end up owning all the shares?

American experience of share schemes which have been running successfully for sixty years is that the total employee shareholding is unlikely to rise as high as 25 per cent of issued share capital, even after all this time. The reason is that employees change jobs, retire or die, or they may have certain reasons for wanting to cash their shares or switch their investments. In Europe, where tradition favours a shorter holding period for employee shares than in the United States, it is unlikely that, over the long-term, employee shareholding will rise even as high as it has in American companies.

The basic mathematics of optimum profit-sharing were completed by a German economist, J. H. von Thunen, who died in 1950, but they were not extensively used until his book was translated into English in 1960. Thunen's concept of an equilibrium point at which employee motivation would be maximised and both shareholders and employees would gain most, has proved to be realistic. His formula has been proved by extensive American practice in companies whose management had never heard of him.

The real significance of Thunen lies in the reassurance that companies are not likely to exceed the equilibrium point of profit-sharing. It is immediately obvious to management, shareholders and employees that they all lose if this equilibrium point is exceeded. In this area, at least, there is now a formula for telling us how not to kill the goose that lays the golden egg.

What, in essence, are the Thunen mathematics?

Every employer is entitled to ask: 'But surely, if I begin to share profits with employees and let them come in on the ownership of some of the company's shares, there will be no end to their demands? They will go on and on until they own the lot.'

In fact, it would be against the employees' own interests to behave in this way. This was shown by Thunen who demonstrated that there is a point of fair division of profits which provides maximum reward for both capital and labour.

Thunen used higher mathematics and he developed a formula $\sqrt{ap}$ for the point of fair shares, but it can now be given a modern interpretation, in terms of simple arithmetic. For those who want Thunen's formula briefly explained, we quote a summary of it presented by the late Professor Joseph Schumpeter of Harvard University in his *History of Economic Analysis*:

For simplicity, consider a one-year production process, the only expense of production being wages. Call the dollar value of the national net product p, the total pay roll w, so that total profits (which Thunen, like others, identified with interest) are $p - w$, and the rate of profits (interest) is $\frac{p-w}{w}$. Suppose that the wage receivers spend a fixed amount, a, per year, investing the rest, $w - a$, at the current rate of interest, $\frac{p-w}{w}$. On this investment, they will evidently earn:

$$\frac{p-w}{w}\,(w-a) = p - w - \frac{ap}{w} + a$$

If this expression is to be a maximum, we must have* (p and a being treated as constants and *d* being the differential)

$$\frac{d\,(p-w-\frac{ap}{w}+a)}{dw} = -1 + \frac{ap}{w^2} = 0$$

from which follows Thunen's formula,

$$w^2 = ap, \text{ or } w = \sqrt{ap}$$

*In order to have a maximum and not a minimum it is further necessary that the second derivative be negative. But this is all right, since it equals $\left(-\dfrac{2ap}{w^3}\right)$, a, p and w being essentially positive. This would maximise workers' income from investment. The idea is not without interesting suggestions and might be used among other things in certain schemes of profit sharing. But, of course, this wage is not 'natural' in the sense that the free market mechanism tends to produce it. The formula does not embody Thunen's theory of wages. Nor is it an essential part of it. The wildly unrealistic assumptions should not, however, prompt us to declare the argument wrong. Under its assumptions it is quite right.

After Thunen had devised his formula for the fair wage, he wrote:

This wage, not originating in the relation of supply and demand, not measured by the needs of the worker, but proceeding from the self-determination of the worker, this $\sqrt{ap}$, I call the natural wage.

Bernard Dempsey, who translated Thunen into English 110 years after his death, after having read Schumpeter, made this comment:

The *natural* wage, as Schumpeter so correctly observed, is not one which will be produced by a market mechanism or emerge by itself from the competitive process. Thunen's natural wage arises out of organisation achieved by the self-determination of voluntary agents as opposed to machines and materials.

Thunen's wage is natural in the sense that it conforms to natural justice. He described the frontier situation in the nineteenth-century United States, where free land could be had at the frontier, so that every worker had the choice of being a capitalist or remaining an employee. In this situation, where an employee chose to remain in employment, deferred profit-sharing gave him the prospect of building up capital in the business on a similar basis to that which he might have achieved if he had moved west to the frontier.

Interpreting Thunen Today
Thunen's formula gives the geometric mean between the consumed part of the reward of labour and the total reward available to capital and labour, or what is now called value added. Thunen, as a disciple of Adam Smith, followed strictly the Smith line that 'capital comes from parsimony'. In other words, before the days of income tax, the whole of profit could be regarded as dividend to be paid out as personal income, then to be saved by reinvestment, or spent. In fact, however, a modern business has already committed the greater part of its profit as investment before the extent of the profit is known.

In a modern economy where deferred profit-sharing is used so that employees may participate in the ownership of any increase in the capital of the company arising from reinvestment of profits, the practical way to interpret Thunen's formula is to look at the end result of a period of capital accumulation by both shareholders and employees. The cumulative end result of a period of sharing on the basis of the geometric mean is likely to be a 50:50 split, for the geometric mean is the dynamic version of the arithmetic mean, for a moving situation.

How is a 50:50 split achieved progressively over a long period, such as a full working life of fifty years? (If a business owner was going to share his capital accumulation 50:50 with labour, he would presumably do this over his full working life, ie, the period in which he was personally responsible for accumulation.) We know from compound interest tables that any number which increases by 1.4 per cent a year doubles itself in fifty years. This gives us a guide as to how fast we can issue shares to employees. For example, if a businessman builds up from nothing a business worth £4 million during his working life of, say, fifty years, and if he is prepared to share the value of the business 50:50 with his employees, he can do this on a continuing basis if he distributes scrip issue shares at the rate of 1.4 per cent of his issued share capital per year.

If a businessman had to raise capital from outside shareholders in the course of building up his business, this would reduce the proportion of shares available to employees. Hence, the rate of scrip issue to employees would have to reduce below the 1.4 per cent per annum maximum.

Experience of many employee share schemes suggests that in most companies the right rate of scrip issue, in public companies at least, is likely to be no more than 1 per cent per annum. This is, in fact, approximately the rate which is acceptable to financial institutions in the City of London.

What percentage of the profits of a business needs to be shared on an annual basis in order to finance the purchase of 1 per cent of the share capital? For simplicity, let us ignore the problems of inflation and taxation. It may then be said that any company which shares 10 per cent of its profits with its employees and is earning profits equal to 11 per cent on its capital will have 10 per cent available to the present shareholders plus 1 per cent to buy new, scrip issue shares for the employees. If the accepted earnings yield on the shares is 10 per cent, then the employees' profit-share will be adequate to buy them scrip issue equal in value to 1 per cent of the issued share capital.

If the company made profits of considerably more than 11 per cent on capital, would the employees receive more shares? Not to any substantial extent, for the shares would go up in price. If the profits were doubled, for example, the shares could be worth twice as much, so that a doubled profit-share for employees would only buy the same number of shares.

What would happen if a company decided, perhaps under pressure from employees or government, that it should share 20 per cent of profits with its employees? In this case, the maximum rate of scrip issue could rise from 1 per cent to 2 per cent per annum. This latter does not seem high as a once and for all figure, but on an annual basis it is absurd. It means employee acquisition of nearly two-thirds of the capital during the working life of the original owners. This is so discouraging to independent investment as to be against the interests of the employees themselves. For example, no employee pension fund could invest in industry on these terms.

There seems to be no escape from the conclusion that the right level of profit-sharing in order to provide maximum return to both capital and labour is the Thunen level. When expressed in simple arithmetic, this is typically no more than 10 per cent of profits and it involves typically no more than 1 per cent per annum scrip issue of shares for employees. These are broad limits. The right figures for a particular company will depend on a number of factors, particularly on the amount of capital per employee and the degree of dependence on the public capital market.

Because employees change jobs, retire or have other reasons for wishing to sell shares of a particular company for which they have worked, any company share scheme which aims to build up a 50 per cent employee shareholding over a period of fifty years, typically builds up no more than a 25 per cent employee shareholding. This has been shown to be the case by sixty years of American share scheme experience. In the longer term, the buy-back of shares from employees reaches an equilibrium level where the total employee shareholding arising from a deferred profit-sharing scheme is unlikely to exceed 25 per cent of the total capital. French government administrators were so impressed by the outcome of American experience, that they put a 25 per cent limit on employee shareholding in nationalised firms, such as Renault, which set up employee share schemes. They argued that, if experience showed that employee shareholding did not, in practice, exceed 25 per cent of total shareholding, why not make this an arbitrary limit and thereby allay any suspicion that employee share schemes were being used to change, in a surreptitious way, the control of industry?

Thus we are able to see a pattern for the future by which thrusting entrepreneurship may live side by side with employee shareholding and with the needs of private citizens and investment institutions, such as unit trusts, pension funds and insurance companies, to invest on behalf of a wide range of citizens:

The entrepreneur, whether an individual or a corporation or a government authority	50 per cent, more or less
The investing public, including private citizens, unit trusts, pension funds and insurance companies	25 per cent more or less
The employees	25 per cent or thereabouts in the longer term

In the larger public companies where the directors exercise the entrepreneurial function and where there may be no dominant shareholding, the pattern is more likely to be as follows:

The investing public, including private citizens, unit trusts, pension funds and insurance companies	75 per cent or more
The employees	up to 25 per cent in the longer term

SOURCE DOCUMENTS

This appendix concludes with the presentation of a number of source documents which tell their own story of the gradual development, within the British civil service and the three major political parties, of an understanding of the need to provide facilities for companies to run deferred profit-sharing schemes which enable employees to accumulate share capital.

In these documents the anonymity of civil servants is respected. There is no point in evading the fact that the author was the management consultant mainly involved, although no advertising takes place in the documents. As for the client company which became the test case, it is now public knowledge that Habitat set up the first deferred profit-sharing scheme in Britain, so the company's name has not been removed from the letters published here.

EXTRACT FROM A LETTER TO A MANAGEMENT CONSULTING FIRM
12.3.75 FROM THE INLAND REVENUE
RE: A CLIENT'S DEFERRED COMPENSATION PLAN

> Inland Revenue
> Somerset House,
> London WC2 1LB

The general question of Schedule E liability under US plans of this type which provide for the deferment of payments, has recently been considered by the Board of Inland Revenue. The Board's view is that liability under Schedule E arises at the time the employer's contribution (the Original Payment) is made but that since the employee has at that time only a contingent right to the Original Payment the actual assessment of contribution should be delayed until the employee acquires an indefeasible title thereto, ie, normally at the end of 3 years. Thus an Original Payment for 1974 will be regarded as assessable for 1974/75 and once the participant has acquired an indefeasible title, ie, normally in 1977 a further assessment for 1974/75 will be made. If a participant leaves his employment before the expiry of 3 years from the making of the Original Payment and obtains an indefeasible right to part of that payment then a further assessment for the year of the contribution will be made at that time.

As I indicated in our recent telephone conversation the Board will, however, allow individual participants to opt for assessment under Schedule E on what might be called the receipts basis. Such an election will be irrevocable. The effect of an election will be that participants will be assessable for the year in which they acquire an indefeasible interest to the Original Payment, ie, normally in the case of a 1974 award in 1977/78. The amount assessable will be the value of the participant's share in the Plan at the time he becomes indefeasibly entitled thereto which may, of course, be a greater or smaller sum than the Original Payment. No doubt you will ensure that participants are aware of the alternative basis of assessment available to them. Any employee who wishes to elect for the receipts basis should forward his election to the Inspector at .... district.

APPLICATION BY A CONSULTANT TO THE BOARD OF INLAND REVENUE FOR ELIMINATION OF DOUBLE TAXATION AND THE FAVOURABLE RESPONSE

11 February 1976

Double Taxation of Employees in Profit-Linked Share Schemes

Some weeks ago, your colleague, Mr . . . gave me your name when it appeared that I might need to discuss unresolved tax points relating to the Habitat Profit-Linked Share Plan (CI3915/75). There are still two points not yet decided. Moreover, the decisions so far made, though not basically unfavourable, nevertheless oblige the client to choose the less desirable course—taxation of participants on an Earnings basis instead of on a Receipts basis. The latter apparently leads to Double Taxation of Employee Income, as outlined in the enclosed memorandum.

This matter was discussed recently at a meeting of the Wider Share Ownership Council and I notice that they have put it in their pre-budget submission to the Chancellor. They are urging the elimination of Double Taxation of Employees.

In view of the urgency of the Habitat case, I am wondering whether the Board of Inland Revenue would prefer to consider this as a matter for concession, rather than legislation? The sums involved are small.

If you feel as I do that we could have a useful meeting on this subject, I shall be happy to come along at a mutually convenient time.

REQUEST TO THE BOARD OF INLAND REVENUE
FOR THE ABOLITION OF DOUBLE TAXATION OF
EMPLOYEES PARTICIPATING IN A PROFIT-LINKED SHARE SCHEME

Under Section 25 paragraph (3) of the Finance Act 1965, Capital Gains Tax is charged on the trustees to settled property when the beneficiaries become absolutely entitled to any settled property. Clearly the architects of this 1965 Act could not have foreseen that a tax designed for inheritors of settled property would, in 1976, impose Double Taxation on Employees participating in a Profit-Linked Share Scheme.

Briefly, a Profit-Linked Share Scheme is one in which a part of the profits of a company is set aside for employees and invested in shares for them, but they cannot sell the shares for a specified period, such as three or five years. This holding period gives them experience as shareholders.

The profit-sharing bonus for employees is allowable as a cost, for corporation tax purposes, and the Inland Revenue is agreeable to deferment of Income Tax until the employee actually has the shares released to him.

The best basis for tax assessment is a 'Receipts' basis. That is, the Revenue agrees to tax only the value of the shares when released. This ensures that if the shares have gone down in value, the employee pays tax only on what he can realise, not on the value of the original bonus invested in shares.

However, during the holding period, the shares are held for the employee by trustees and they are regarded by the Revenue as being held by 'trustees to settled property', so that under Section 25(3) of the Finance Act 1965, Capital Gains Tax has to be charged on the Trustees as well as Income Tax on the employees. In effect, therefore, there is Double Taxation and this could not have been intended in 1965.

One way to avoid this is to have employees taxed on an 'Earnings' basis, but this puts the employee at risk of receiving less from the sale of his shares than the tax assessed on his original bonus. There is also a tax liability on the Trustees if the employee holds on to his shares after the end of the holding period and they fall in value.

Undoubtedly, the best method of running this type of employee share scheme is on a 'Receipts' basis, but as mentioned above, this means Double Taxation. The Board of Inland Revenue is requested to agree, as a concession, to waive the Capital Gains Tax on the Trustees.

LETTER FROM THE INLAND REVENUE TO A CONSULTANT

12 April 1976

Double Taxation of Employees in Profit-Linked Share Schemes

Mr . . . has asked me to write to you on the Capital Gains aspects of the request for concessional treatment which was contained in the memorandum enclosed with your letter of 11th February. I must apologise for the delay which has occurred in replying to your letter but, as you will be aware from your telephone conversations with Mr . . . , this matter has been under close review. It has also been considered by my colleague in relation to the Capital Transfer Tax aspects and I understand that he will be writing to you within the next few days.

I can now confirm that in practice we are prepared to relieve the trustees of the charge to Capital Gains Tax under Finance Act 1965 s25(3) when a director or employee becomes absolutely entitled as against those trustees to shares which were settled property, and the director or employee has been assessed on the Schedule E 'receipts' basis under ICTA s181 on the market value of those shares at the date of absolute entitlement.

There will be circumstances in which the gain assessable upon the trustees under FA 1965 s25(3) will be subject to reduction under the provisions of FA 1972 s79(9) by the amount chargeable under s79(4). However, the trustees will be permitted to forego the deduction of that amount in favour of the employee in order that they can be relieved of the s25(3) charge under the practice described in the previous paragraph. The employee will then be able to claim a deduction of the amount chargeable under s79(4) in the Capital Gains computation on his disposal of the shares.

I hope that this practice will provide a solution to the 'Double Taxation' problem to which you have drawn my attention.

LETTER FROM THE INLAND REVENUE TO A CONSULTANT
Habitat Profit-Linked Share Plan

15 April 1976

I am now able to reply to your letter of 14th January asking about the effect of the above plan in relation to Capital Transfer Tax. I am sorry that it has not been possible to reply more quickly.

The first thing to be said is that for the purpose of this tax each Original Payment will constitute a separate settlement made by the company under the combined effect of the

Trust Deed and the relevant written directions under Clause 2. I understand that the payment by the company will be allowable for the purpose of Corporation Tax on the company's profits. On this footing and on the assumption that the provisions in the current Finance Bill replacing paragraph 9 of Schedule 6, Finance Act 1975 are duly enacted, I can confirm that these payments will not be taxable as transfers of value made by the company, notwithstanding that it appears to be a close company.

The application of the further exemptions given by paragraph 17 of Schedule 5 of that Act depends on whether the condition in sub-paragraph (2) is satisfied in relation to the Original Payment concerned. That condition requires that those eligible to benefit from the payment as Qualifying Employees within the definition in Rule 2.8 then comprise more than 50% of the total employees of the company.

If paragraph 17 does not apply to the settlement of any particular Original Payment there will be a potential charge for Capital Transfer Tax under paragraph 6(2) of Schedule 5 when a participant becomes entitled to his share of the Payment under Rule 9 or Rule 11.1 of the Scheme. But where the protection of paragraph 17 is available such claims will be restricted to payments made to those referred to in sub-paragraph (4) of that paragraph.

EXTRACT FROM HANSARD

Statement in the House of Commons, London, by the Minister of State, Treasury (Mr Denzil Davies), 4 February, 1977, when replying on behalf of the Government to the introduction of a Private Member's Employee Investment Bill by Mr Julian Ridsdale, MP.

The Government do not disapprove of private share ownership. Nor do we disapprove of the Bill because it allows greater ownership of shares in industry. Indeed, the contrary is true. Nothing we have done inhibits greater ownership of shares by workers in industry—indeed, there are many schemes in existence. There is nothing to prevent the extension of share ownership by employees in the industry in which they work—indeed, it is happening all the time in British industry. We are not against the Bill for that reason. We are against it because of the reasons given so clearly by my hon and learned Friend the Member for Hackney, North and Stoke Newington (Mr Weitzman). At the end of the day, this is not a Bill to promote wider share ownership by employees in industry; it is a tax Bill.

The Bill seeks to make major changes, for good or ill, in tax legislation. Opposition Members have spoken at length about the benefit of these provisions as a result of ownership of shares. Clause 3 was hardly mentioned, and without that clause the Bill is of no use. That clause, which is the crux of these provisions, refers to

'any shares . . . or any interest in shares . . . acquired in pursuance of a scheme to which this Act applies'

and then refers to

'any benefit received by any person by virtue of the ownership of or interest in the shares acquired under the scheme'.

The whole success of the Bill depends on Clause 3, yet there has been no discussion about the effect of that clause on our tax laws. Undoubtedly it involves a major change in legislation.

That comprises the Government's opposition to the Bill. If this has to be carried out as a major form of change, it will have to be instituted by means of provisions in the Finance Bill instead of by a Private Member's Bill, however worthy its aims may be.

219

EXTRACT FROM A CONSERVATIVE GREEN PAPER ON
PERSONAL CAPITAL BUILDING AND WIDER
PARTICIPATION IN THE CREATION OF WEALTH—SOME PROPOSALS
A Consultative Document
March 1977

Part II
The Scheme in Detail

i) *Employee Tax Relief.* Our proposals are based on improving the tax position of profit sharing schemes. We build on the existing provision whereby companies are free to pay employee bonuses whether provided in shares or cash from profits and to deduct these as a normal cost before corporation tax. The snag is that the employees themselves suffer income tax on their bonuses, calculated either on an 'earnings' or a 'receipts' basis. Our proposal would substitute for the present charge to income tax a tapered deferred tax confined to employee bonuses given in shares and derived from profits.

ii) *Tapered Tax Rate.* The taper period would be confined to an absolute maximum of five years. The rate would, of course, depend on decisions on income tax and capital gains tax generally. Our broad thinking is that there be a minimum holding period of two years, except for death or circumstances involving enforced and permanent retirement when the holdings could be withdrawn at the basic rate of income tax; in the third year 20 per cent tax would be levied on encashments; the fourth 15; the fifth 10; and holdings for a full five years would be completely free of all tax due up to that point. Shareholders could then either retain their shares, whose current market price at that time would be the base value for capital gains tax on a subsequent sale; or sell for cash, perhaps reinvesting in other shares or assets. In many cases it might be possible to use the sale proceeds as deposit on a house.

220

iii) *Safeguards.* As a safeguard against excess revenue cost or distortion of the scheme, we propose that companies should not be able to set aside more than say, 10 per cent of their pre-tax profits for share bonus schemes; that consideration be given to some limit on overall company contributions to all the various kinds of tax-relieved benefits, on US lines; and that no individual should have allocated on his behalf more than £1,000 a year—a figure which would need to be reviewed annually. Substantial shareholding in a firm by an individual would exclude his participation in a scheme run by that firm. The scheme would, of course, be voluntary. Each company would be free to determine the details of individual benefit and the pattern of share allocation. Schemes attracting the deferred tax relief proposed would be required to apply to the majority of a firm's employees; it would be up to individual companies to decide whether or not to introduce such a scheme.

iv) *Smaller Companies.* Although at first sight the above arrangements might appear to be most suitable for quoted companies, smaller companies, if they so wish, can certainly make use of the potential advantages. Broadly similar schemes have been adopted by numerous smaller and unquoted companies in the United States. Apart from the choice of direct equity shareholding, share profits could be distributed to employees in the form of loan stock maturing after five years, while carrying rights to equity participation in the event of the company going public or resolving in general meeting to effect such participation within a similar (or perhaps rather longer) period.

v) *Qualifying Trusts.* The unit and investment trust movement could have an important part to play in accelerating the spread of capital ownership through deferred profit share schemes. Initially we suggest that unit and investment trusts would be relieved of all capital gains tax on disposals in 'participation companies'—that is to say companies operating employee share ownership schemes. (This tax concession would be analogous to capital gains tax relief on sales of gilt-edged stocks held for more than one year.) Later, specialist trusts with most of their assets in such companies could be developed. The potential attractiveness of such investment, owing to the capital gains tax relief, would facilitate fund raising by participating companies.

vi) *Legal and Administrative Aspects.* While we are anxious to get shares to the individual at the earliest possible moment, appointment of trustees would be necessary:

1 To receive from the company the allocation of shares and hold them on behalf of employees for up to five years (we envisage that they would be fully vested after that time).

2 To administer the tax deduction on sales within the five year period—we envisage that 'deferred income tax' would be operated on a simple tapered tariff, with no personal reliefs, and that trustees would pay out a net sum to vendors.

3 To receive dividends (net of basic rate tax) and either accumulate them or (if preferred) reinvest them on behalf of the employees.

4 To provide a means, in any necessary consultations with management of representing the interests of beneficiaries. It would be important for beneficiaries to be directly represented amongst the trustees (or amongst the directors of the trustee company, when relevant).

It would be a condition of the scheme that trustees could invest only in the shares of the company in question. It is possible that companies would normally require a minimum period of service before employees entered a scheme—say two years—so that any administrative complication from rapid job turnover would be eliminated.

vii) *Cost.* It is not possible to calculate precise Exchequer cost of the reliefs involved in the above proposals, since this would depend on the speed of take up of the scheme, the part played over time by profit shares in the total 'remuneration package', and the timing of disposals of shares by employees. We believe however that the cost, narrowly calculated in potential revenue foregone, would be small in the first and second year, and in practice would be negligible. The final outcome would almost certainly be a net gain in revenue flows arising from a healthier economy.

EXTRACT FROM A SPEECH BY MR DAVID STEEL, MP
AT A LIBERAL PARTY CONFERENCE, BRIGHTON, 28.9.77

I propose three steps to break down the barriers in industry. First, I believe that the transition from a rigid pay policy should not be the total free-for-all of free collective bargaining. The encouragement of genuine plant productivity deals in which employees get a direct share in the rewards from increased output should become the pattern for greater prosperity in the 1980s.

Second, we favour a total but calm and not hasty review of the whole framework of labour legislation which should include new measures to promote a genuine working partnership in industry.

Third, I want to see as part of a programme based on first creating and then sharing greater wealth, direct encouragement of profit sharing and employee shareholding schemes. In our agreement for the next session of Parliament the Government undertook 'to consider ways of encouraging the creation of profit sharing in private industry with a view to legislation'.

Work has been proceeding in the Treasury on this subject and the Government has been in consultation with the Liberals on possible tax incentive schemes. The Chancellor has told me that he intends to issue a consultative document outlining these within the next three months and that, provided all goes well, the necessary legislation will follow in next year's Finance Bill*.

*At the time of this book going to press, the 1978 Finance Bill contains provisions for tax relief on participants in an employee share scheme of the type described in this Appendix, when the participants hold their shares for at least five years.

Appendix III

Presentation of Figures to Non-accountants

WHAT IS GOING ON IN THE BUSINESS?
A WORKING MODEL OF THE UNIVERSAL MONITORING SYSTEM

Nobody can play his part very happily in a budgeting and review system unless he knows where the figures he is using came from. Therefore this appendix devotes considerable space to showing budget and actual statements relating to virtually all the main aspects of a business and in the notes explaining each statement there is given the most usual source, in the formal accounting system, of the figures used.

These budget and actual statements are presented in a deliberately provocative manner to highlight some of the most important problems of a business which, if not considered frequently and dealt with promptly, can wreck it. They present a logical way in which a person without accountancy training can discover, through figures, what is going on in a business.

This pattern of reports, with provocative headings, is presented in the order listed below. It concludes with one showing how personal progress can be laid out in the same manner as company progress.

Subjects covered

Fig 23 Are your sales adequate? Is your order book going up or down?

Fig 24 Are customers paying their bills? Are you paying yours? How much cash is in the kitty?

Fig 25 How much have you spent on that marketing campaign? How fast are you recovering the costs?

Fig 26 Are your weekly sales (or bookings) satisfactory?

Fig 27 Are your various projects on schedule?

Fig 28 How fully are you using your firm's capacity?

Fig 29 How short-staffed are you?

Fig 30 How fast are stocks being used?

Fig 31 Are you keeping production costs in check? How much have you got invested in raw materials?

Fig 32 How much have you got invested in work in progress, finished goods, machines and buildings?

Fig 33 What are your delivery costs? How much have you got tied up in delivery vehicles and depots?

Fig 34 Are your overhead costs in line?

Fig 35 How much is being accrued and written off or depreciated for office capital costs?

Fig 36 Are you running at a profit each month? How well have you done this year so far? How well have you done over the years?

Fig 37 What is the net worth of the business in the balance-sheet? How is this represented by share capital and loans?

Fig 38 How well is that new project going?

Fig 39 What are the future prospects for the business? What is its future cash position likely to be?

Fig 40 How is the self-financing productivity scheme progressing?

Fig 41 What sort of progress is Mr Jones making within the company?

SALES REVENUE AND ACCRUED ORDERS		1	2	3	4
Product A		43,000	39,000	42,000	51,000
		39,100	40,500	39,800	
Product B		17,000	31,000	34,000	39,000
		24,900	34,500	39,700	
Total Sales		70,000	70,000	76,000	90,000
		64,000	75,000	79,500	
			140,000	216,000	
			139,000	218,500	
	Opening order book plus	181,400	192,000	194,400	
The	Orders rec'd less	74,600	77,400	85,600	
order	Invoiced sales	64,000	75,000	79,500	
book	Closing order book	192,000	194,400	200,500	

Figure 23 Are your sales adequate? Is your order book going up or down?

APPENDIX III

Notes on Figure 23

1 Sales revenue means invoiced sales and/or cash sales. The goods have actually been produced and delivered and either invoiced or paid for.
2 The sales revenue figures will come from the sales day book, which may be in two parts, invoiced sales and cash sales. In the day book all sales are entered in the order in which they occur.
3 Invoiced sales will also be entered in the sales ledger accounts of each customer who runs an account. Thus, the total of sales during the month, as entered in these ledger accounts, should equal the total of invoiced sales recorded in the sales day book. Checking these totals is one way of locating errors.
4 Orders should be recorded in the order book only when they are firm orders—usually in writing. Some businesses can supply customers immediately but some take months or even years to produce what the customer wants, either because it has to be specially made, such as an oil tanker, or because it is only economic to produce a particular item in batches and the time has not yet come for producing the next batch of the item specified. It may be a particular weave of textile or a particular colour and model of motor car.
5 Wherever there is a lag between receipt of orders and fulfilment, the order book provides valuable evidence of the state of the business. If, for example, the total of outstanding orders is increasing, this may be due to a rising level of orders or to failure of the production department to fulfil orders.
6 The actual level of invoiced sales of product A is running mostly below the budgeted level, while the actual level of invoiced sales of product B is running mostly above the budgeted level. When the two are totalled, it is found that cumulatively, invoiced sales for the first three months are slightly ahead of budget.
7 The outstanding level of unfulfilled orders is typically equal to about three months' sales, but the orders being received are regularly ahead of invoiced sales. There is an overall rising level of demand for the company's products but the production department is failing to keep up wth rising demand, though it is performing well enough to achieve the original budget figures.
8 The opening order book at the beginning of any month is the same as the level of orders at the end of the previous month, ie it is the same as the previous closing order book. Thus, the closing order book at the end of January is £192,000 and the opening order book at the beginning of February is also £192,000. To this opening order book is added the value of new orders received and from this total is then deducted the value of invoiced sales, to produce the closing order book, or level of outstanding orders at the end of February.

Notes on Figure 24

1 The company's creditors are those to whom the firm owes money for supplies or services rendered but not yet paid for. By adding up all the unpaid bills entered in the bought ledger, one arrives at a total of outstanding creditors. This should check with the total of unpaid bills in the purchases day book.
2 To the opening total of creditors one adds the total of invoices received during the month, as totalled in the purchase day book, and then one deducts the total of payments sent out to suppliers during the month, as shown in the cash book. This should provide the closing level of creditors. The total of cheques paid out to suppliers, as shown in the

cash book, should tally with the total of items marked off as paid in the ledger accounts of the various suppliers, in the bought ledger.

3 The company's debtors are those who owe the firm money for goods or services bought from it but not yet paid for. By adding up the unpaid items in the sales ledger, one arrives at a total of outstanding debtors. This should check with the total of unpaid items in the sales day book.

4 To the opening total of debtors one adds the total of invoiced sales for the month, as totalled in the sales day book, and then one deducts the total of payments received from customers during the month, as shown in the cash book. This should provide the closing level of debtors. The total of cheques received from customers, as shown in the cash book, should tally with the total of items marked off as paid in the ledger accounts of the various customers, in the sales ledger.

5 The company's cash is the cash in the bank. We are not concerned here with petty cash which will be supplied regularly in bulk to various administrative staff and recorded as bulk items of expenditure. They will then keep the detailed accounts of how it is spent. The company's cash position is recorded in the cash book, where payments in and out, concerned with the daily operations of the business, will be recorded in separate columns. There will then be other columns for occasional special items, such as receipt or repayment of a bank loan, or receipt of additional capital from the owners of the business, or for the purchase and sale of items of capital equipment.

6 Because there will be some cheques being processed which have been entered in the company's books but have not yet been recorded in the bank's books, it is not easy to reconcile the company's cash book with the bank statement. One has to prepare a reconciliation statement listing all those cheques recorded by the company and not yet recorded by the bank, and vice versa, adding or deducting these totals, as appropriate. The advanced method of avoiding reconciliation, used by companies with computers, is for the company's computer to be programmed to list out on tape all the payments which the company wishes to make. The tape is then passed to the bank which puts it through its own computer, the payments are made and a new bank statement is prepared. Thus, in effect, the bank's computer is keeping the company's cash book. The bank supplies the company not only with a list of payments made but also with a list of payments received, so that this tape can be passed through the company's computer and debtors can be credited with the amounts they paid.

7 Assuming that the problem of reconciliation has been overcome, one can then add to the opening bank balance the total of cash paid in, as shown in the cash book, and deduct the total of cash paid out. This should give a closing bank balance. The cash book will, of course, record moneys paid in and out for cash transactions as well as for sale or purchase of goods on credit.

8 The cash balance at the bank may be negative, if arrangements have been made in advance for the account to be overdrawn, or the company may have obtained a bank loan, which is paid into the operating account and this account reads positive even though the company is in debt to the bank.

CREDITORS, DEBTORS AND CASH		31/1	28/2	31/3	
	Opening creditors plus Invoiced expenditure	1170,000	150,000		
		32,000	27,840		
	less Payments made	52,000	20,840		
	Closing creditors	150,000	157,000		
	Opening debtors plus Invoiced sales	100,000	106,000		
		64,000	75,000		
	less Payments received	58,000	61,000		
	Closing debtors	106,000	120,000		
	Opening bank balance plus Cash paid in	31,800	37,800		
		58,800	61,000		
	less Cash paid out	52,000	20,840		
	Closing bank balance	37,800	77,960		

Figure 24 Are customers paying their bills? Are you paying yours? How much cash is in the kitty?

		1	2	3	4	5	6
Salesmen's salaries		6,000	6,000	6,300			
		6,100	6,100				
Salesmen's expenses		1,500	1,500	1,600			
		1,600	1,650				
Advertising & promotion		1,800	1,800	2,100			
		1,750	1,710				
Sales	overheads	700	700	700			
		750	740				
Total	selling costs	10,000	10,000	10,600			
		9,000	11,000				
Opening vehicle value plus		40,000	41,800				
New purchases		2,500	–				
less Sales and depreciation		700	750				
Closing vehicle value		41,800	41,050				
Opening advertising accruals plus		–	4,250				
New advertising expenditure		6,000	3,000				
less Expenditure taken into costs		1,750	1,710				
Closing advertising accruals		4,250	5,540				

Figure 25 How much have you spent on that marketing campaign?
How fast are you recovering the costs?

231

APPENDIX III

Notes on Figure 25

1 Selling involves at least three types of expenditure:

   a The salary cost and expenses of the people actually selling.
   b The cost of advertising and promotion.
   c The cost of maintaining an administrative office, wth all the usual overheads that cannot be directly attributed to specific sales.

2 Some of the costs have to be incurred all at once, although they are intended for write-off over a period. For example, a salesman's car may be written off over five years. It would greatly distort the selling costs if the whole cost of the car were charged to the month in which it was purchased. Likewise, an advertising campaign may be carried out at the beginning of the season but it is intended to accrue most of this expenditure and charge it as a cost during successive months of the season.

3 This table shows salesmen's salaries and expenses, advertising and promotion costs, sales overheads, and finally total selling costs. In the salesmen's expenses will be some depreciation of their cars. Further down is shown a running account of the value of sales vehicles, with the addition of new purchases and the subtraction of depreciation and money obtained from selling old vehicles. The depreciation subtracted in the lower half of the table will be included in the salesmen's expenses in the top half. Any money obtained from selling old vehicles increases the company's cash, shown in the balance sheet, just as money needed to buy new vehicles decreases the cash.

4 At the bottom of the table is shown a running account of the advertising and promotion expenditure which has been accrued. Any new expenditure which is not intended to be charged as an immediate cost is added to this total and from it is deducted the month's share of the season's campaign cost, thus producing a new total of accruals. The month's share of the campaign cost must be taken in as a cost of advertising and promotion, entered in the top half of the table.

5 Any sales manager presented with such a table can see immediately how his expenditures are progressing compared with budget, and how fast he is writing off the capital costs, such as vehicles and advertising, incurred by his operation.

6 Sales overheads may well be broken down under detailed headings on a separate sheet, as shown in Figure 34, for company overheads. Some of these overheads will involve capital items, such as office furniture, which will have to be depreciated and shown in a running, or roll-over account. However, we are concerned here only with illustrating typical items, not with presenting the full figures for every department of a business. Your accountant will advise on how to handle all the items relevant to your business and he will set up the necessary systems.

WEEKLY SALES, IN UNITS			6.1.78	13.1.78	20.1.78	
Product K			5,000	4,500	5,000	
			5,174	4,952	5,175	
				9,500	14,500	
				10,126	15,301	
Product M			200	210	220	
			211	217	223	
				410	630	
				428	651	

Figure 26 Are your weekly sales (or bookings) satisfactory?

Notes on Figure 26

1 It has already been mentioned on p 81 that planning and control sheets have thirteen columns, not twelve, because some firms like to set out their figures in four-week periods, of which there are thirteen in a year, instead of in calendar months. Another reason given for having thirteen columns is that there are some figures, particularly sales figures in the consumer goods manufacturing and retail industries, which need to be reported weekly. If there are thirteen columns, each column can be used for a week's figures and the thirteen columns will cover a quarter.
2 It is possible to compare the weekly progress of eight products against budget on the one sheet, or the weekly takings of eight departments in a retail shop, or the weekly bookings for eight different holiday packages, and so on.
3 Each of the weekly figures may need to be cumulated, for although it may be vital to watch weekly progress and take quick action if sales fall or rise rapidly, there are many reasons, such as public holidays, bad weather or major public events, which can interfere with sales or bookings in any one week but which may not affect the seasonal trend, as shown by cumulating the figures from week to week.
4 There are also many physical measures of activity, such as tonnes of steel delivered or cartons of product K sold, which need to be recorded and monitored on a weekly basis, for which the thirteen column sheet is very useful.

233

WEEK	BY	WEEK	COMPARISON	OF	ACTUAL	PERFORMANCE	AGAINST
				1	2	3	4
Project A					DESIGN	20/1	DEVELC
						18/1	

Figure 27 Are your various projects on schedule?

ROOM BOOKINGS						
Week ending		6.1.78	13.1.78	20.1.78		
Hotel X		700	700	700		
		436	597	285		
Hotel Y		420	420	420		
		317	256	398		

Figure 28 How fully are you using your firm's capacity?

ACTUAL STAFF COMPARED WITH ESTABLISHMENT					
Week ending		6.1.78	13.1.78	20.1.78	
Dept A		15	15	15	
		12	13	12	
Dept B		24	24	24	
		19	20	20	

Figure 29 How short-staffed are you?

234

6	7	8	9	10	11	12	13
10/2	STAGE 1 PRODUCTION	23/2	STAGE 2 PRODUCTION	8/3	COMPLETION		27/3
12/2		27/2					

Notes on Figure 27

1 Following on from the notes to Figure 26, it may be said that a third reason for having thirteen columns on a planning and control sheet is to provide for time scheduling and the comparison of performance against schedule.

2 The schedules for eight different projects may be laid out, week by week, using the shaded rows for scheduling, as is also done for budgeting. Each stage of a project is shown with a dotted line and its end point is marked with the date for scheduled completion of the stage.

3 Beneath the schedule is shown actual performance, each stage being shown with a continuous line drawn on the clear space and its end point marked with the actual date of completion of the stage.

4 Thus it is easy to compare actual performance against schedule and to photocopy the sheet periodically and circulate copies to all concerned.

5 There are on the market more sophisticated types of planning charts which are built in A4 sections so that each section can be unslotted from its wall-board and put on a copying machine.

Notes on Figure 28

1 Following on from Figures 26 and 27, a fourth reason for having thirteen columns on a planning and control sheet is to provide for the comparison of actual usage of facilities against the capacity available.

2 It may be a comparison of used machine-time against actual time available or airline seats sold against the number available or beds occupied against the number available or vehicle-days hired out against the number available, and so on.

3 Such comparisons usually need to be assessed and reported weekly, if they are going to be useful in reaching decisions on changes in policy which may be urgently needed.

4 The capacity available is shown on the shaded area, as with budgets and schedules. The actual usage is shown on the clear area, as with any other type of actual performance.

5 Usage of capacity may have to be shown cumulatively as well as week by week in order to observe any trends.

Notes on Figure 29

1 Following on from Figures 26, 27 and 28, a fifth usage of a thirteen-column sheet is to provide for the comparison of actual resources available against the planned level. The most usual case is to compare the number of actual people employed in each function or department against the agreed and planned 'establishment'.

235

2 If a department is under-performing, one of the first things to check is whether they are short of staff. The same table enables one to check whether they are over-staffed.

3 As would be expected, the planned and agreed establishment figures for each department are shown on the shaded areas and the actual staff numbers are shown on the clear areas.

4 The figures cannot be cumulated, so it would be possible to present sixteen different departments on the one sheet, although eight would be better, leaving space in between.

		1	2	3	
Item A	Opening stocks plus				
		4,654	4,858	3,226	
	New supplies less				
		2,000	-		
(number)	Usage and spoilage				
		1,796	1,632		
	Closing stocks	4,858	3,226		
Item B	Opening stocks plus	974	922	996	
	New supplies				
		-	150		
(tonnes)	less				
	Usage and spoilage	52	76		
	Closing stocks	922	996		

Figure 30 How fast are stocks being used?

Notes on Figure 30

1 The running record, or roll-over system, as illustrated on the bottom of Figures 23 to 25, can be used as in Figure 30 to record the levels and movements of physical stocks of any type.

2 'Physical stocks' means the actual number of items or weight or volume of an item, in contrast to the money value of stocks, shown in earlier tables.

3 To the opening stocks are added the new supplies and from this total is subtracted the amount used or written off as spoilt, to obtain the closing level of stocks. This then becomes the opening level for the next period.

236

	1	2	3	4	5	6	
duction wages	12,000	12,000	12,800				
	11,100	13,400					
erials	10,000	10,000	10,900				
	9,300	10,700					
vices	3,000	3,000	3,300				
	2,900	3,100					
rheads	5,000	5,000	5,000				
	4,700	4,800					
al production costs	30,000	30,000	32,000				
	28,000	32,000					
ning stocks of raw erials							
ıs	30,000	35,700					
purchases							
ss	15,000	–					
erials used and tten off							
	9,300	10,700					
sing material cks							
	35,700	25,000					

Figure 31 Are you keeping production costs in check? How much have you got invested in raw materials?

Note on Figure 31

1 The main production costs are: wages, including social service and other contributions; raw material costs; services such as heat, power, light, water and cleaning; administrative overheads such as production manager's office, rent and salary costs, etc, and also depreciation on buildings and machines.
2 This table shows these items and also total production costs.
3 At the bottom of the table is a roll-over account of the value of raw material stocks. Each month one can see the opening value, to which is added the value of new purchases. From this is deducted the value of materials used and any which have to be written off due to spoilage, thus giving a closing value of raw material stocks.
4 The value of materials used, shown at the bottom of the table, must be taken in as a cost and entered at the top of the table. The value of materials written off may be treated as a special item, if it is seriously large, in the company's overall profit and loss account, where it will be explained in a footnote.

Notes on Figure 32

1 In the roll-over account of work in progress, to the opening level will be added all new expenditure on production which does not directly lead to completed goods. From this total will be deducted the value of completed goods taken into stock or sold. Thus, the closing level of work in progress is arrived at.
2 In the roll-over account of finished goods, to the opening level will be added the value of all completions of goods (which were formerly work in progress) and then will be deducted the value of goods sold from stock. This gives the new closing value of finished goods.
3 In the roll-over account of machines, to the opening level will be added the value of new purchases and from this total will be deducted depreciation on all machines and the value of any machines sold. This provides the new closing value of machines. The rate per month at which a company depreciates its machines, in order to charge them as a cost (eg one-sixtieth per month over five years) may be slower than is allowed for tax purposes. The faster rate of depreciation for tax purposes will reduce the company's immediate tax bill and hence conserve its cash for further capital expenditure.
4 In the roll-over account of buildings, to the opening level will be added the value of new purchases and new construction and from this will be deducted depreciation, in cases where they can be depreciated, and also the value of any sales of buildings, to give the new closing level in value of buildings. If there has been a revaluation of buildings, this will also have to be taken into account.
5 All depreciation on machines and buildings deducted in this table must be charged as a production cost, under production overheads, as shown in Figure 31.

		1	2	3	
WORK IN PRO-GRESS	Opening level plus	111,000	90,000		
	New expenditure	28,000	32,000		
	less Completions	59,000	71,000		
	Closing level	90,000	51,000		
FIN-ISHED GOODS	Opening level plus	135,500	140,500		
	Completions	59,000	71,000		
	less Goods sold	64,000	75,000		
	Closing level	140,500	144,500		
M A C H I N E S	Opening level plus	211,300	190,300		
	New purchases	-	21,700		
	less Depreciation and sales	21,000	24,000		
	Closing level	190,300	226,600		
B U I L D I N G S	Opening level plus New purchases and construction	266,600	260,100		
		-	3,610		
	less Depreciation and sales	6,500	6,500		
	Closing level	260,100	257,210		

Figure 32 How much have you got invested in Work in Progress, Finished Goods, Machines and Buildings?

239

		1	2	3	
	Delivery wages	2,000	2,000	2,200	
		1,900	2,050		
	Vehicle costs	1,500	1,500	1,600	
		1,350	1,550		
	Depot costs	1,000	1,000	1,100	
		800	950		
	Overheads	500	500	500	
		450	450		
	Total delivery costs	5,000	5,000	5,400	
		4,500	5,000		
V E H I C L E S	Opening value plus	20,000	22,700		
	New purchases less	3,000	–		
	Depreciation and sales	300	350		
	Closing value	22,700	22,350		
D E P O T S	Opening value plus New purchases & construction	40,000	39,900		
		–	2,000		
	less Depreciation and sales	100	110		
	Closing value	39,900	37,790		

Figure 33 What are your delivery costs? How much have you got tied up in delivery vehicles and depots?

Notes on Figure 33

1 The main delivery costs are shown: wages, vehicle running costs, warehouse running costs and overheads, and also total delivery costs.
2 In the lower half of the table are roll-over accounts for vehicles and warehouses, including depots. Any depreciation deducted in these accounts must be entered as a cost in the top half of the table.

		1	2	3	
	Personnel	6,500	6,500	6,500	
		6,400	6,450		
	Premises	1,500	1,500	1,500	
		1,550	1,500		
	Telephone	150	150	150	
		140	150		
	Office supplies	200	200	200	
		190	210		
	Office mailing	200	200	200	
		180	190		
	Insurance	50	50	50	
		50	50		
	Professional fees	150	150	150	
		100	160		
	Travel	130	130	130	
		120	120		
	Entertaining	20	20	20	
		15	25		
	Cars (running costs)	300	300	300	
		335	315		
	Depreciation	500	490	480	
		500	490		
	Interest	150	150	150	
		150	150		
	Royalties	100	100	100	
		100	100		
	Miscellaneous	50	60	70	
		20	40		
	TOTAL	10,000	10,000	10,000	
		9,500	10,000		

Figure 34 Are your overhead costs in line?

Notes on Figure 34

1 Typical items of overhead costs are listed in this table, but the actual items entered for any particular business will vary with the nature of the business.
2 If premises are rented, the cost of premises will include rent and rates, heating, lighting and other services, such as cleaning and porterage.
3 Depreciation will apply to furniture, machines, vehicles and, in some cases, buildings.

241

		1	2	3	4
R O Y A L T I E S	Opening accrual plus	300	400	500	60
	Standard accrual	100	100	100	
	less Actual payment	-	-	540	
	Closing accrual	400	500	60	
F U R N I T U R E	Opening value plus	9,000	8,850	8,701	
	New purchases	-	-		
	less Depreciation and sales	150	149		
	Closing value	8,850	8,701		
M A C H I N E S	Opening value plus	10,465	12,600	12,500	
	New purchases	2,412	-		
	less Depreciation and sales	205	201		
	Closing value	12,710	12,399		
C A R S	Opening value plus	8,585	8,440	8,300	
	New purchases	-	-		
	less Depreciation and sales	145	140		
	Closing value	8,440	8,300		

Figure 35 How much is being accrued and written off or depreciated for office capital costs?

		1	2	3		
	Sales revenue	70,000	70,000	76,000		
		64,000	75,000			
	Other revenue					
	TOTAL REVENUE	70,000	70,000	76,000		
		64,000	75,000			
	Selling costs	10,000	10,000	10,600		
		9,000	11,000			
	Production costs	30,000	30,000	32,000		
		28,000	32,000			
	Delivery costs	5,000	5,000	5,400		
		4,500	5,000			
	Overhead costs	10,000	10,000	10,000		
		9,500	10,000			
	TOTAL COSTS	55,000	55,000	58,000		
		53,000	58,000			
	PROFIT OR LOSS	15,000	15,000	18,000		
		11,000	17,000			
R	Opening level plus	720,000	731,000			
E S	New profit or less	11,000	17,000			
R	New loss					
V E S						
	Closing level	731,000	748,000			

Figure 36 Are you running at a profit each month? How well have
you done this year so far? How well have you done over
the years?

243

	31/1	28/2		
Fixed assets	300,000	295,000		
Other durable assets	241,000	256,000		
Current assets	410,000	424,000		
less				
Current liabilities	150,000	157,000		
New current assets	60,000	67,000		
NET WORTH	801,000	818,000		
Share capital subscribed	50,000	50,000		
Loan capital subscribed	20,000	20,000		
Reserves	731,000	748,000		
TOTAL CAPITAL	801,000	828,000		

Figure 37 What is the net worth of the business in the balance sheet? How is this represented by share capital and loans?

APPENDIX III

Notes on Figure 35

1 Items such as royalties or interest may be payable periodically, eg, every six months, and the exact amount may not be known, either because the payment depends on sales volume, as in the case of royalties, or because interest rates change. Nevertheless, some provision must be made for future payment. Therefore, an estimated sum is accrued every month and charged as a cost. At the end of the six-month period there will hopefully be only a small adjustment to make to the monthly payment to enable the total actual charge to be competely written off.
2 Furniture, machines and cars are typical items of capital cost for an office which need roll-over accounts so that one can see how much capital is tied up in them, and also how fast it is being depreciated and charged as a cost.

Notes on Figure 36

1 All revenue and cost items are brought together so that total revenue and total costs can be seen, and hence the balance of profit or loss. This can be shown both monthly and cumulatively.
2 The cumulative figure of past profits, or reserves, is shown at the foot of the table in a roll-over account.

Notes on Figure 37

1 Here in outline is the balance-sheet, ignoring certain important complications which accountants have to worry about, such as special reserves to meet future taxation liabilities.
2 The value of fixed assets, as currently depreciated, is shown as well as the value of other durable assets, eg furniture, vehicles and machines.
3 The current assets consist of the value of stocks (both raw and finished) and work in progress, plus debtors (ie money owed by customers) plus cash, if there is any.
4 The current liabilities consist of the creditors (ie, money owed to suppliers) plus loans or bank overdraft.
5 Deducting current liabilities from current assets, one obtains the net current assets. When these are added to the fixed and other durable assets, one has the net worth of the business, as shown in the balance-sheet.
6 Lower down in the table is shown the share capital subscribed by the shareholders and also the loan capital subscribed. The reserves are also shown for, as we saw earlier, the profit of a business is the same thing as the increase in capital, if we ignore taxation and dividends. Any profit left in the business after deducting taxation and dividends is added to the reserves, for it represents an increase in the capital left with the business by the shareholders. Any dividends they receive are a reward for leaving their capital with the business for yet another year.
7 When the share capital subscribed plus loan capital subscribed plus reserves are added, to obtain the total capital, we should have a figure which is the same as the net worth. This is the meaning of a balance-sheet: the two parts balance. The money put in by the suppliers of capital plus the reserves they have left in the business must be equal to the sum of its assets. If they are not, a mistake has been made in the accounts, possibly by entering a figure up wrongly or failing to enter it up. The professional disciplines undertaken by accountants, in the course of arriving at a 'balanced' balance-sheet, are a most important element in the maintenance of human liberty, for they enable people to put trust in those who operate independent enterprises, to which independent resources have been loaned or subscribed.

245

PROJECT 'A' CASH FLOW	1	2	3	4	5	6	7
Revenue	50	55	47	59	61	63	
	51	58	53				
Cash inflow from operations	25	48	53	50	56	60	61
	23	47	54				
Operating expenditure	40	43	48	48	57	50	
	41	48	58				
Cash outflow from operations	26	39	41	45	46	49	48
	25	38	42				
Capital expenditure	60	25	10	10	-	-	
	65	23	11				
Cash outflow from capital expenditure		55	30	20	1		
		57	28				
NET CASH INFLOW	-1	-46	-18	-25	+9	+11	+13
	-2	-48	-16				
		-47	-65	-90	-81	-70	-57
		-50	-66				

Figure 38 How well is that new project going?

Notes on Figure 38

1 Quite apart from looking at a company's operations as a whole, it may be desirable to look at specific projects, particularly if they are new projects involving the launching of a new product or service, or the opening of a new branch.

2 This table shows the expected and actual revenue from a new project. Immediately below the revenue figures are cash-flow figures. When revenue is invoiced, customers may not pay their bills for at least a month. Therefore, it is necessary to adjust the revenue figures by moving them sideways to allow for the time-lag in actually receiving cash.

3 Operating expenditure is shown and, beneath it, the cash outflow for operations, after allowing for delays by the company in paying its bills.

4 Capital expenditure on the project is also shown and, beneath it, cash outflow. If a major structure is being erected, for example, payments may be agreed at certain stages. These must be allowed for.

5 At the bottom of the table is shown the net cash inflow. This may be negative for many months or years, ie, the project may cost the company

246

capital before it brings in any net inflow. These net figures will be cumulated and the cumulative net outflow in any month shows how much capital is being used in the project. Budget figures will be entered up before the project commences and then the actual figures will show progress against budget, month by month.

6 The highest net cumulative outflow figure shows the greatest amount of the company's capital which the project is expected to use (if we are looking at budget figures) or has used (if we are looking at actual figures).

PROJECTED CASH FLOW OF THE BUSINESS	1	2	3.	4
Revenue	70,000	70,000	76,000	
	64,000	75,000		
Cash inflow from operations	60,000	70,000	72,000	74,000
	59,172	69,453		
Operating expenditure	55,000	55,000	58,000	
	53,000	58,000		
Cash outflow from operations	54,000	56,000	53,000	57,000
	51,500	55,065		
Capital expenditure	8,000	26,000	14,000	
	7,912	26,310		
Cash outflow from capital expenditure	4,000	8,000	26,000	14,000
	3,065	4,783		
NET CASH INFLOW	+2,000	+6,000		
	+4,607	+9,615		
		+8,000		
		+14,222		

Figure 39 What are the future prospects for the business? What is its future cash position likely to be?

247

Notes on Figure 39

1 This is the same type of table as Figure 38, except that all the activities of the company are put together and projected over the months ahead.
2 All budgeted revenue is converted into expected cash inflow.
3 All budgeted operating expenditure is converted into expected cash outflow.
4 All budgeted capital expenditure is converted into expected cash outflow.
5 The result is to produce budget figures for overall cash inflow (or outflow, if negative) and from this, cumulative figures of net cash inflow or outflow.
6 This does not, however, tell the whole story unless the cumulative figure of net inflow is supported by the net cash balance of the company at the end of the previous period and this can be added in. Only when it is added in will the cumulative figure show the total prospective cash position of the company in the months ahead. Whether reality will be as good as the prospect remains to be seen.
7 Once the total prospective cash position is known, a pro forma balance-sheet can be constructed, which is an estimated balance–sheet for a future date.

INCREASING PROFITABILITY

INCREASING VALUE ADDED

	-5	-4	-3	-2	-1	0	1	2	3	4	5	6	7	8	9	10	11	12
12	3·2	3·8	4·3	4·9	5·4	6·0	6·6	7·1	7·7	8·2	8·8	9·4	9·9	10·5	11·0	11·6	12·2	12·7
11	2·7	3·3	3·8	4·4	4·9	5·5	6·1	6·6	7·2	7·7	8·3	8·8	9·4	9·9	10·5	11·0	11·6	12·2
10	2·2	2·8	3·3	3·9	4·4	5·0	5·6	6·1	6·6	7·2	7·7	8·3	8·8	9·4	9·9	10·5	11·0	11·6
9		2·3	2·9	3·4	4·0	4·5	5·0	5·6	6·1	6·7	7·2	7·8	8·3	8·9	9·4	9·9	10·5	11·0
8			2·4	2·9	3·5	4·0	4·5	5·1	5·6	6·2	6·7	7·2	7·8	8·3	8·9	9·4	9·9	10·5
7				2·4	3·0	3·5	4·0	4·6	5·1	5·6	6·2	6·7	7·2	7·8	8·3	8·8	9·4	9·9
6					2·5	3·0	3·5	4·1	4·6	5·1	5·6	6·2	6·7	7·2	7·8	8·3	8·8	9·4
5						2·5	3·0	3·6	4·1	4·6	5·1	5·6	6·2	6·7	7·2	7·7	8·3	8·8
4						2·0	2·5	3·0	3·5	4·1	4·6	5·1	5·6	6·2	6·7	7·2	7·7	8·2
3							2·0	2·5	3·0	3·6	4·1	4·6	5·1	5·6	6·1	6·6	7·2	7·7
2								2·0	2·5	3·0	3·6	4·1	4·6	5·1	5·6	6·1	6·6	7·1
1									2·0	2·5	3·0	3·5	4·0	4·5	5·0	5·6	6·1	6·6
0										2·0	2·5	3·0	3·5	4·0	4·5	5·0	5·5	6·0
-1											2·0	2·5	3·0	3·5	4·0	4·4	4·9	5·4
-2													2·4	2·9	3·4	3·9	4·4	4·9
-3														2·4	2·9	3·3	3·8	4·3
-4															2·3	2·8	3·3	3·8
-5																2·2	2·7	3·2

THE FIGURES IN THE SQUARES ARE EMPLOYEE BONUS AS A PERCENTAGE OF PAY

Figure 40 How is the self-financing productivity scheme going?

Notes on Figure 40

1 The bonus grid relates both value added and profitability to employee bonus.

248

Born . . . . Name . . . .

Joined . . . . Address . . . .

National Insurance No . . . .

EMPLOYEE PAY AND BENEFITS RECORD		1976	1977	1978	1979		
	Job title	Sales Mgr.	–do–				
	Department	Sales	Sales				
	Salary scale points	402	413				
	Point value	£20	£21				
	Salary or wage	8,040	8,673				
	Bonus earned	570	780				
	Bonus accrued	–	140				
	PAID	570	650				
	Special allowances	–	–				
	Total earnings	8,610	9,323				
	Pension prospect	33/60	33/60				
	Life cover	4xSal	4xSal				
	Health insurance·	–	–				
	Car	Cortina	–do–				
	Loan	200					
			100				
	Share allocation	150	170				
			320				

Figure 41 What sort of progress is Mr Jones making within the Company?

249

2 The vertical axis of the bonus grid measures the change in the ratio of value added to employee costs between the previous period and the period being measured.

3 The horizontal axis measures the variation of the profitability of the company in the previous period from a pre-determined norm.

4 Where the vertical and horizontal measures intersect, employees can read off their bonus, expressed as a percentage of pay.

5 The equation behind the grid, which is specific to the company and its circumstances, involves one or more 'hunting factors' which determine the rate at which bonus levels improve as the company's operations improve.

6 It is obvious to employees, at a glance, that they share a common interest with the company in keeping it operating in the top right-hand corner of the grid, where both bonuses and profits are maximised.

7 Typically, the total grid is broken into two—a cash bonus grid and a deferred bonus grid.

8 The bonus grid smooths out the fluctuations in bonus which arise in Rucker-type value added incentive systems and at the same time it guarantees to the company's finance director that there will be no excessive drain on his cash resources when profits are high.

9 This is a truly 'self-financing' system, with no bonus payable unless there has been an improvement in performance over the pre-bonus situation.

Notes on Figure 41

1 This table assumes that a self-financing productivity deal of the kind described in Chapter 14 was in operation during the period of the pay-increase limit imposed in Britain from 1975 to 1977.

2 Any forecast or anticipated salary will be entered on the shaded background. Actual salary is on the clear background.

3 Allowances may include special cost-of-living allowances.

4 Bonus may include some provision for carry-forward if a ceiling is reached.

5 Total earnings must likewise provide space for carry-forward.

6 Pension prospect, life cover, health insurance and car require a mere mention, in brief, as to whether or not the benefit is provided and, if so, a rough indication of scale. The pension benefit should be summed up in terms of what fraction of final pay the employee will ultimately get at normal retirement age. The prospect of permanent ill-health is roughly as great as the prospect of dying in service and coverage against these eventualities is important to many people.

7 Loan facilities, such as for education, need to be set out so that new drawings are clearly seen and also the cumulative net position, after allowing for pay-backs.

8 Share allocations also need to be set out so that new allocations are clearly seen and also the cumulative position of shares allocated, but in this case ignoring disposals, which are a personal matter, though forfeitures must be deducted.

9 As payrolls are perhaps the most computerised section of business, experimental programming work on computerising Figure 41 is a natural point of entry into the computerising of a universal monitoring system for the company.

Bibliography

Argyle, Michael. *Social Interaction* (Methuen, 1969)

Berne, Eric. *Games People Play* (André Deutsch, 1966)

Blumberg, Phillip. *The Megacorporation in American Society: The Scope of Corporate Power* (Prentice-Hall, 1975)

Calder, Nigel. *The Human Conspiracy* (BBC Publications, 1976)

Child, Dennis. 'The Relationship Between Introversion and Extraversion, Neuroticism and Performance in School Examinations' (*British Journal of Education Psychology*, June 1964)

Copeman, George. *The Challenge of Employee Shareholding* (Business Publications, 1958)

Dempsey, Bernard. *The Frontier Wage* (Loyola University Press, 1960)

Eysenck, H. J. *Experiments in Personality* (Routledge, 1960)

Furstenberg, Fredrich. *Why the Japanese have been so successful in Business* (Leviathan House, 1974)

Galbraith, J. K. *American Capitalism* (Penguin, 1952)

Goffman, Erving, *The Presentation of Self in Everyday Life* (Pelican, 1969)

Greenwalt, Crawford H. *The Uncommon Man* (McGraw-Hill, 1955)

Haberland, Gunther. *Crisis Management* (Leviathan House, 1975)

Harris, Thomas. *I'm O.K., You're O.K.* (Random House, 1971, Jonathan Cape, 1973)

Hertsberg, F. *Work and the Nature of Man* (Crosby Lockwood Staples, 1968)

Kelso, Louis D. and Adler, Mortimer J. *The Capitalist Manifesto* (Random House, 1958)

251

Keynes, John Maynard. *The General Theory of Employment, Interest and Money* (Macmillan, 1936)

Leber, Georg. 'Accumulation of Assets for the Worker' (*Schriftenreihe Der Industriegewerkschaft Bau-Steine-Erden* [in English] 1964)

Lewin, Roger. 'The Brain's Other Half' (*New Scientist*, 6 June 1974) (*see* Ornstein, Robert E.)

Lowe, Sir Toby (later Lord Aldington), *Everyman a Capitalist* (Conservative Research Centre, 1958)

McClelland, D. C. *The Achieving Society* (The Free Press, 1967)

McCracken, Paul, and others. *Towards Full Employment and Price Stability* (OECD, 1977)

McGregor, Douglas. *The Human Side of Enterprise* (McGraw-Hill, 1960)

McLuhan, Marshall. *Gutenberg Galaxy* (Routledge, 1962)
—— *Understanding Media* (Routledge, 1964)
—— *The Medium is the Message* (Penguin, 1971)

Marshall, Alfred. *Principles of Economics* (first published 1890; Macmillan, 1966)

Marx, Karl. *Capital* (first published 1886; George Allen & Unwin, London, 1946)

Mepham, G. 'Pay: Why It Is Wrong to Discriminate Against Discretion' (*The Times*, 20 October 1976)

Metzger, B. L. *Pension, Profit-sharing or Both?* (Profit-sharing Research Foundation, 1975)
——and Colletti, J. A. *Does Profit-sharing Pay?* (Profit-sharing Research Foundation, 1970)

Morgan, E. Victor. *Personal Savings and Wealth in Great Britain* (Financial Times Publications, 1975)

Moynihan, Daniel Patrick, 'How much does freedom matter?' (*Atlantic Monthly*, July 1976)

Nothdurft, K. H. *Business Negotiation* (Leviathan House, 1974)

Ornstein, Robert E. *Psychology of Consciousness* (Jonathan Cape, 1975) (*see* Lewin, Roger)

Prais, S. J. 'A New Look at the Growth of Industrial Concentration' (lecture to City University, 20 March 1973)

Raw, Charles. *Do you Sincerely Want to be Rich?* (André Deutsch, 1971)

Royal Commission on 'The Distribution of Income and Wealth, First Report' (HMSO, 1975)

Sales Force Info, fortnightly sales training newsletter (Leviathan House, London)

BIBLIOGRAPHY

Schumpeter, Joseph A. *History of Economic Analysis* (Oxford University Press, 1959)

Smith, Adam. *An Enquiry into the Nature and Causes of the Wealth of Nations* (first published 1776; Penguin, 1970)

Soldofsky, Robert M. *Institutional Holdings of Common Stock 1900–2000* (University of Michigan, 1971)

Speiser, Stuart M. *A Piece of the Action* (Van Nostrand Reinhold, 1977)

Stern, Philip. *The Rape of the Taxpaper* (Random House, 1973)

Thunen, Johann Heinrich von. *The Isolated State, Part II* (*see* Dempsey, Bernard)

Wage, J. *The Successful Sales Presentation* (Leviathan House, 1974)

Wood, Adrian *A Theory of Profits* (Cambridge University Press, 1975)

Zielke, W. *How To Put Method Into Your Thinking* (Leviathan House, 1974)

Acknowledgements

I am particularly grateful to Herr Wolfgang Dummer of Munich for opening a window on to some remarkable developments in German and North European management practice. I am also indebted to Professor Peter Moore of the London Business School for helping me to see my way through self-financing productivity systems for paying employees. Very many thanks to Mrs Joan Strachan for such meticulous attention to detail when typing and retyping my manuscript. Finally, I am extremely grateful to my wife for her repeated reading of the MS to help me clarify it.

The work sheets were typed by Shirley Cotton.

253

Index